PENGUIN CLASSICS

THE AMERICAN DEMOCRAT

JAMES FENIMORE COOPER (1789–1851) was born in Burlington, New Jersey. He was the son of a prosperous landholder who founded Cooperstown in New York state near the Canadian border, where he spent his youth. Educated at Yale, he left without graduating and after a brief period in the navy, he embarked on a career in writing. Although primarily renowned in Europe as a 'Frontier' writer and as the author of *The Last of the Mohicans* – especially famed is his Leatherstocking or Hawkeye series – he was also a recognized social critic. His own personal involvement in politics from childhood days led to a stormy career upon his return to America from Europe in 1833, after which he became a tirelessly severe critic of his own country. Towards the latter part of his life there was a distinct fusion of satire, social criticism and romance in his novels. By his death it was difficult to say whether he was mainly a romantic story-teller, or a brilliant, penetrating student of democracy in action.

•

GEORGE DEKKER has been Professor of English at Stanford University, California, since 1974. A specialist in English and American Romanticism, American poetry and American historical literature, he is the author of *Sailing After Knowledge: The Canto of Ezra Pound, James Fenimore Cooper the Novelist, Coleridge and the Literature of Sensibility*, and co-editor, with John McWilliams, of *James Fenimore Cooper: The Critical Heritage*. He has also written many articles and reviews on these and other American writers.

•

LARRY JOHNSTON was a lecturer in the Department of Government at Essex University and specialized in American government and politics in the School of Comparitive Studies. He is co-editor of *The President: Roles and Powers*.

THE
AMERICAN DEMOCRAT

JAMES FENIMORE COOPER

Edited with an introduction by
George Dekker and Larry Johnston

PENGUIN BOOKS

PENGUIN BOOKS

Published by the Penguin Group
27 Wrights Lane, London W8 5TZ, England
Viking Penguin Inc., 40 West 23rd Street, New York, New York 10010, USA
Penguin Books Australia Ltd, Ringwood, Victoria, Australia
Penguin Books Canada Ltd, 2801 John Street, Markham, Ontario, Canada L3R 1B4
Penguin Books (NZ) Ltd, 182–190 Wairau Road, Auckland 10, New Zealand

Penguin Books Ltd, Registered Offices: Harmondsworth, Middlesex, England

First published 1838
Published in Pelican Books 1969
Reprinted in Penguin Classics 1989
1 3 5 7 9 10 8 6 4 2

Made and printed in Great Britain by
Hazell Watson & Viney Limited
Member of BPCC Limited
Aylesbury, Bucks, England
Set in Intertype Georgian

CONTENTS

INTRODUCTION

THE NOVELIST AS POLITICAL THEORIST

'HAD a suitable compound offered,' writes Cooper in his introduction to *The American Democrat*, 'the title of this book would have been something like "Anti-Cant". . . .' Less arresting, less obviously true to the spirit of the book, 'The American Democrat' is a more informative and comprehensive title. More informative, because this is a book about the theory and practice of democracy in America. More comprehensive, because in Cooper's usage 'American Democrat' subsumes 'Anti-Cant'. For one of the chief aims of the book is to provide a model of the way an authentic American democrat would think and speak – without cant – on the subject of the American democracy:

By candor we are not to understand trifling and uncalled for expositions of truth; but a sentiment that proves a conviction of the necessity of speaking truth, when speaking at all; a contempt for all designing evasions of our real opinions; and a deep conviction that he who deceives by necessary implication, deceives wilfully.

In all the general concerns, the publick has a right to be treated with candor. Without this manly and truly republican quality, republican because no power exists in the country to intimidate any from its exhibition, the institutions are converted into a stupendous fraud.

An American democrat, then, is by definition a truth-teller. As for the institutions themselves, 'truths, moral, political, and social, are peculiarly the aim of this government'. But one of the central and agonizing truths he has to tell his fellow-Americans is that the majority of them neither know, face, nor speak the truth about themselves or their institutions. Instead, 'the voice of simple, honest, and what, in a country like this, ought to be fearless, truth, is nearly smothered . . .'

On this showing, the political institutions of the United States had indeed been converted into a 'stupendous fraud', and the real American democrats reduced to a nearly helpless minority. While Cooper stopped short of a diagnosis so drastic and self-defeating, he did nevertheless believe that cant and lack of candour were rapidly destroying the health of the American body politic. The truth as he saw it, 'simple' and 'fearless,' was a scalpel to cut out that disease. Often enough, the truth as he saw it was altogether too simple. But then as now in America, in spite or because of the popular institutions, it was not easy to be fearless in stating the truth from a minority point of view. Cooper knew well the price of dissent, and he had to pay dearly for insisting on his right and responsibility to call a spade a spade. *The American Democrat* is above all a courageous book, exhilarating and bracing because its author is as candid as we should all like to be – if only we had his moral nerve.

But if a passionate commitment to the truth can account for the moral authority, it cannot account for the intellectual distinction of *The American Democrat.* Nor can it explain how James Fenimore Cooper, best known as the author of *The Last of the Mohicans* and other fantastic tales of wilderness adventure, came to write this richly informed minor classic of American political theory. Not commitment to truth, but fascination with its opposite – deception – is perhaps the clue we are after. As a novelist, Cooper himself was a practitioner of the art of (innocent) deception, of *vraisemblance*; and we need only look into one of his Leatherstocking tales to discover how obsessed he was with various kinds of deception: for instance, the disguises, the treacherous oratory, the ingenious ruses and ambushes of his bad Indians. At times, indeed, he seems to have had an almost childish addiction to 'make believe'. Yet like Plato before him, Cooper was worried about the moral and epistemological status of an art of 'imitation' – something which was not the 'real thing'. He once remarked: 'all fictions are dangerous in their nature. . . .'* Clearly even his own works of fiction could not escape from such a categorical stricture. But admitting this to be the case, what has it to do with politics? A great deal. For Cooper's remark was prompted, not by a reflection on literature, but by an observation that the British Government (in 1830) was ostensibly a constitutional monarchy but was effectively an aristocracy. Preoccupied as he was with deception, he could not fail to be deeply interested in politics: for, as he comments in *The American Democrat*, 'nothing can be less alike than governments ordinarily are, in their action, and in their professions'. And the general run of politicians seemed to him devious, when not unscrupulously designing, men. Given this view, the connexion between his literary and political concerns must be clear. For him, literature and politics were equally absorbing studies, and for much the same reasons.

What Cooper brings to the study of politics, then, is a moralist's commitment to truth and a novelist's preoccupation with the discrepancy between appearance and reality, profession and practice, names and things. Both qualities are apparent in *The American Democrat*, but, as we might expect, they are even more obviously present in his political fiction. Probably his greatest political novel is *The Bravo* (1831), a work which portrays the old republican government of Venice as a soulless 'monied corporation' of aristocrats who pretend to rule in the interests of the people as a whole, but who in fact rule for themselves and maintain their power only through bribery, assassination, and an elaborate network of spies and secret police. *The Bravo*, though in its way an impressive portrait of a totalitarian

Letters and Journals of James Fenimore Cooper, ed. J. F. Beard, Jr (Cambridge, Mass., 1960–68), Vol. II, p. 107.

regime, is highly melodramatic. So was Cooper's view of politics at the time he wrote it. For he was then deeply involved in the plans and intrigues of liberal European politicians at a critical moment in history – when a wave of revolutionary activity swept across Europe, leading in England to the Reform Bill, in France to the July Revolution, and in Poland to abortive uprisings against the Tsar. *The Bravo*, though ostensibly a portrait of old Venice, was almost certainly a disguised commentary on the contemporary governments of England, France, and Russia. Faced with the possibility that his political views would be censored in Europe, Cooper himself was using a form of literary duplicity to publish an attack on what he considered a right-wing conspiracy against popular rights.

The American Democrat was published seven years later, when Cooper had become more cynical about reform movements and less prone to see a conspiracy behind every political development that displeased him. Nevertheless, a preoccupation with deception in one or another of its manifestations does govern much of the analysis in this book. For example:

Men are the constant dupes of names, while their happiness and well-being mainly depend on things. The highest proof a community can give of its fitness for self-government, is its readiness in distinguishing between the two; for frauds, oppression, flattery and vice, are the offspring of the mistakes.

Or we might well return to the problem with which we began: how is it that the 'truly republican quality' of candour is so little practised, is indeed so very difficult to practice, in the American republic? Says Cooper: 'It would be a singular and a false effect of freedom, to destroy a nation's character for candor; but we are not to be deceived by names, it being quite possible that a tyranny of opinion should produce such results, even in a democracy.' Or rather, as he goes on to show, *especially* in a democracy:

In this country, in which political authority is the possession of the body that wields opinion . . . there is a strong and dangerous disposition to defer to the publick, in opposition to truth and justice. This is a penalty that is paid for liberty, and it depends on the very natural principle of flattering power. In a monarchy, adulation is paid to the prince; in a democracy to the people, or the publick. Neither hears the truth, as often as is wholesome, and both suffer for the want of the corrective. The man who resists the tyranny of a monarch, is often sustained by the voices of those around him; but he who opposes the innovations of the publick in a democracy, not only finds himself struggling with power, but with his own neighbors. It follows that the oppression of the publick is of the worst description, and all real lovers of liberty, should take especial heed not to be accessories to wrongs so hard to be borne. As between the publick and individuals, therefore, the true bias of a democrat, so far as there is any doubt of the real merits of the controversy, is to take sides with the latter. This is opposed to the popular notion, which is to fancy the man who maintains his rights against the popular will, an aristocrat, but it is none the less true. . . .

The last sentence is a good example of 'Anti-Cant', and the entire passage exemplifies his persistent effort to trace political deception and self-deception to their sources. The results of his researches, though doubtless fascinating to Cooper the novelist, were scarcely gratifying to Cooper the moralist: to govern themselves or others, men needed precisely that faculty which they were least likely to develop in a hurry; for the 'ability to discriminate between that which is true and that which is false, is one of the last attainments of the human mind'.

To be a moralist and at the same time a novelist writing about politics is not without its perils. The moralist, if his moral vision have any intensity, is apt to magnify a weak and perhaps slightly crooked political opponent into a devil. The novelist is likely to dramatize muddle into machination. Cooper does both at times, and when he does he tends to substitute rhetoric or literary stereotype for political analysis – as in his characterization of a demagogue:

The demagogue is usually sly, a detractor of others, a professor of humility and disinterestedness, a great stickler for equality as respects all above him, a man who acts in corners, and avoids open and manly expositions of his course, calls blackguards gentlemen, and gentlemen folks, appeals to passions and prejudices rather than to reason, and is in all respects, a man of intrigue and deception, of sly cunning and management, instead of manifesting the frank, fearless qualities of the democracy he so prodigally professes.

This is not much more convincing than one of the stage Machiavels of Elizabethan times, and it is less entertaining. But in general, Cooper recognizes that 'Power always has most to apprehend from its own illusions', more to fear from its own follies than from the intrigues of its enemies. He perceives that politicians are rarely deliberate liars; rather, 'Most of the political men of the day belong to this class of doubtful moralists, who, mistaking a healthful rule, which admonishes us that even truth ought not to be too offensively urged, in their desire to be moderate, lend themselves to the side of error.' Even these relatively temperate opinions might be censured as revealing a mind which is excessively, indeed misleadingly, suspicious. After all, how can Cooper always be sure that 'doubtful moralists', when saying things that strike him as equivocal or erroneous, are not merely confused, or speaking in haste, or more correct than Cooper as an outsider can possibly appreciate? But it is better in such matters to be too suspicious than too trusting. The great virtue of *The American Democrat* is that it so rarely accepts things at their face value. Like his great Indian-fighter hero Hawkeye, Cooper is always on the lookout for an ambush or a secret snare; and he can hardly be blamed if, now and again, he is taken in by the wiles or blunders of other American democrats, who themselves

supposed that they were hot on the trail of a false democrat – of an arrogant American aristocrat named James
Fenimore Cooper.

THE PERSONAL CONTEXT

Democrat or aristocrat? This was a question which Cooper's
contemporaries frequently asked not only about him but
also about the leading politicians and political parties of his
day. Cooper himself would have said that the question was
misleading, since – strictly speaking – there were no American aristocrats by birth, few by conviction, and in any case
he was not one of them. But people rarely think or speak
very strictly when they use such labels, and in the America
which was soon to replace 'aristocratic' Martin Van Buren
with a 'Log Cabin' president (Whig General William Henry
Harrison) the confusion over terminology sometimes
amounted to a kind of national political lunacy. Free hard
cider and torchlight parades doubtless had much to do with
the confused vision of American voters during the giddy
campaign of 1840. But even a sober man might be pardoned
for wondering whether, when he gazed at James Fenimore
Cooper, he saw an old-fangled democrat or a new-fangled
aristocrat. True, there was no American aristocracy in the
European sense of a hereditary class with legally guaranteed
social and political privileges. But then as now there was a
class whose inherited wealth made social status and political
influence comparatively easy to come by: to this class
Cooper belonged by birth, education, and marriage. And
therefore, though he might give vigorous support to Andrew Jackson and come to regard Thomas Jefferson as 'the
greatest man we ever had'*, Cooper's allegiance to democracy resulted not in simple enthusiasm but in a powerful
and complex tension between conservative and radical impulses. Out of this tension grew some confusion on Cooper's

*Letters, I, 411.

own part, especially about the social implications of his political doctrines; but it also generated the shrewd critique of democracy and its rival systems that we find in *The American Democrat.*

James Fenimore Cooper's father was William Cooper of Otsego Hall, pioneer founder of Cooperstown, New York, and twice a U.S. Representative during the administrations of Washington and John Adams. Though a man of the people himself (and one who appreciated many of their virtues), Squire Cooper was also an ambitious soul who aimed to establish a dynasty in Cooperstown. His untiring enterprise and benevolent paternalism created a manor house and a family fortune to go with it; his politics, the socially conservative but economically dynamic politics of Alexander Hamilton and New York Governor John Jay, were calculated to secure and extend what had been built. He became one of the most active and partisan Federalist politicians in the state of New York at a time when men of property and high social station apprehended that the revolutionary flames in France might travel all the way across the Atlantic. As a local judge, Cooper enforced the Alien and Sedition laws so vigorously as to cause a scandal; as a congressman, he joined in the Federalist attempt to elect Burr rather than Jefferson by exploiting a defect in the presidential election machinery. Nor is it surprising that William Cooper and many of his Federalist friends were willing to resort to such means. In their apocalyptic vision of American politics, Thomas Jefferson figured as a lurid composite of Don Quixote and Robespierre cheering on the Republican rabble to desecrations of property, religion, and good manners. Or, as James Cooper later reported, 'I was brought up in that school where his [Jefferson's] image seldom appeared, unless it was clad in red breeches, and where it was always associated with the idea of infidelity and political heresy'*. Tame as the Jeffersonian revolution

Letters, I, 95–6.

turned out to be in practice, the violence of American party politics did eventually kill William Cooper: he met his death at the hands of a political opponent who struck him from behind as he was leaving a heated debate in Albany.

Squire Cooper belonged to the heroic, rough-and-tumble phase of American history – a phase that was to be frequently repeated, of course, as the nation moved westward – and he was very happily and successfully a man of his place and time. Times changed and so did the ways of his heirs, but not quite as the Squire planned. James Cooper was brought up to be an American gentleman – which in anglophile Federalist terms meant as nearly an English gentleman as was consistent with a firm belief in the American Constitution. His principal teacher before he went up to Yale was an English clergyman, later described by Cooper as follows:

This man was an epitome of the [English] national prejudices, and, in some respects, of the national character. He ... entertained a most profound reverence for the King and the nobility; was not backward in expressing his contempt for all classes of dissenters and all ungentlemanly sects; was particularly severe on the immoralities of the French revolution, and, though eating our bread, was not especially lenient to our own ... detested a democrat as he did the devil; cracked his jokes daily about Mr Jefferson and Black Sal, never failing to place his libertinism in strong relief against the approved morals of George III. ...*

The gentlemanly influence of this tutor did not prevent young Cooper from getting himself rusticated from Yale a few years later. But after a brief career in the U.S. Navy, Cooper took a step which should have confirmed him, beyond hope, as an anglicized country gentleman: he married a daughter of John Peter De Lancey, an old Harrovian who had himself fought against American independence and

* *Gleanings in Europe: England.*

whose family had long led the royalist faction in York Colony politics. Thus allied with the Tory De Lanceys, patronized by such distinguished Federalist leaders as John Jay and his sons, generously provided for by his beloved father, Cooper was precisely the sort of person egalitarian editors had in mind when they denounced 'American aristocrats'. To be sure, his inherited anglophilia seems not to have survived the War of 1812, and in 1820, after the break-up of the Federalist party, he became an active supporter of the Republican faction led by DeWitt Clinton. But Clinton was scarcely less patrician than Cooper's old Federalists heroes; moreover, he adopted many of their projects for internal improvement (most notably the Erie Canal). In the absence of a viable alternative, conservatives like Cooper joined Jefferson's old party but continued to resist efforts to liberalize voting rights. In 1821, at the age of thirty-two, he was less rigidly partisan than his father but also much more entrenched in the provincial gentry. Time, it seemed, could only make him more reactionary and remote from the popular political movements of the day.

That it did not must be attributed mainly to his fabulous early success as a novelist. After a relatively unsuccessful first book (an imitation of Jane Austen), Cooper wrote *The Spy* (1821), a best-selling tale of the American Revolution which immediately established him as a patriot and literary genius – not merely William Cooper's son, Susan De Lancey's husband or John Jay's young friend, but the famous American novelist James Fenimore Cooper. Moving to New York City, he soon became the centre of a group of literary and political men who represented a much wider range of information and opinion than he had previously encountered. Two of the poets in this group, FitzGreene Halleck and James K. Paulding, were destined to hold Cabinet posts under Democratic administrations; while a third, William Cullen Bryant, besides being the first important American poet, also later became the influential editor of the strongly pro-Jackson *New York Evening Post.* Their comparatively radical views were balanced, however, by those of other members of Cooper's inner circle: for example, the redoubtable Federalist jurist Chancellor James Kent. Cooper himself stood somewhere between these factions, which for the time being were on drinking and speaking terms with each other at both the local and the national levels. But there is some evidence to suggest that he was moving steadily if slowly to the left. In 1825 he followed up the success of *The Spy* with another romance of the American War of Independence, *Lionel Lincoln.* As is customary in English and American novels of this period, the hero of the work is a member of the upper classes, in this case an aristocratic British army officer of American birth but English education who has strong sympathies with both sides. The fictional conventions have, so to speak, a built-in prejudice in favour of the upper classes; but this does not preclude sympathetic treatment of the lower classes, and indeed both *The Spy* and *Lionel Lincoln* are openly appreciative of the courage and patriotism of ordinary ungenteel Americans. What is new in *Lionel Lincoln* is Lincoln's discovery that 'the people' have a political maturity that his aristocratic training had made him suppose impossible:

'Men on the threshold of rebellion seldom reason so closely, and with such moderation. Why, the very fuel for the combustion, the rabble themselves, discuss their constitutional principles, and keep under the mantle of law, as though they were a club of learned Templars.'
'Think you that the fire will burn less steadily because what you call the fuel has been prepared by the seasoning of time?' returned Ralph. 'But this comes from sending a youth into a foreign land for his education! The boy rates his sober and earnest countrymen on a level with the peasants of Europe.'

Cooper himself had received his education on native soil, all right, but it was an education modelled on the one Lionel

Lincoln had received in England. And now, like Lincoln, he was beginning to perceive how blinkered his political education had been. As the quoted passage suggests and as Cooper was to stress in *The American Democrat*, some of the worst blunders have been those committed by men who supposed that what held true politically for Europe necessarily held for America as well – and vice versa. It is a lesson, apparently, which has to be relearned by every generation.

Nevertheless, a first-hand experience of European political movements and institutions was not to be rejected as irrelevant to the interests of a patriotic American democrat, and in 1826 Cooper began a seven-year residence in Europe which intensified his political interests and confirmed his liberalism. Basing himself in Paris, he became the friend and protégé of one of the great heroes of the American Revolution, for many years a leader of the Liberal party in France – the Marquis de Lafayette. A legend in America, Lafayette repaid the affection and veneration of his 'adopted countrymen' by extolling the United States as the polar star of liberty, the practical demonstration that republican principles worked. He welcomed Cooper as a fellow-publicist of the liberal cause – as well he might, since the author of *The Spy* and the early Leatherstocking tales had done more than a dozen ambassadors to create European sympathy for Americans and American ways. Under Lafayette's tutelage and often in his defence, Cooper entered the lists of international political controversy.

At least two of his non-literary efforts to influence the direction of European politics should be mentioned here. The first was his formation of an American-Polish Committee in Paris to gain funds and publicity for the abortive revolution which took place in Poland during the winter of 1830–31. Lafayette was the organizer of a similar French-Polish Committee, and, thanks to the friendship between him and Cooper, the two groups worked closely together to

help the Polish patriots. This support of the brave, tragic
Poles did not injure Cooper's popularity at home, since, in
spite of the cordial relations between the Russian and American governments, the American people generally sympathized with the Polish cause. Less satisfactory was the
outcome of his participation in the so-called Finance Controversy of 1831–2. The controversy was over the respective costs
of republican and monarchical forms of government, with
Lafayette as leader of the Liberals arguing that the United
States government was run more cheaply than the French.
As a visitor in France, Cooper was reluctant to become
involved in a fierce internal dispute between the opposition
party and the government; however, when called upon by
Lafayette, he felt obliged to compile and publish a comparative statistical analysis which demonstrated that Lafayette was right. This enraged the government journals and
provoked disapproving editorials in conservative newspapers
at home. For the first Cooper was of course prepared, but
the second he had not expected. Neither did he expect that
an attaché of the American Ministry in Paris, one Leavitt
Harris, would publicly answer him, arguing that the French
form of government was actually cheaper than that of the
country he represented! Harris's superior, the American
Minister W. C. Rives (a southern aristocrat), maintained a
discreet but equivocal silence which in effect supported his
underling's claims. Cooper recognized that Rives's position
was a difficult one, but he believed that he and Lafayette
had been let down badly by their fellow 'republicans'. His
suspicion that the American government did not take sufficient care to assure the ideological purity of the representatives it sent abroad was dramatically confirmed when
Leavitt Harris was promoted to chargé d'affaires to the
French court. This episode was not forgotten by Cooper: it
is alluded to in *The American Democrat*.

It was also at Lafayette's suggestion that Cooper wrote
his first lengthy book on American democracy – this in the

form of a series of letters about America written by an imaginary European nobleman and published under the title *Notions of the Americans*. Written in 1827, the *Notions* was designed to correct the misimpressions of America created (deliberately or otherwise) by European travellers with an anti-American bias. As an attempt to restore the balance, it concentrates on those sections of the country – New England and the middle Atlantic states – which Cooper not only knew best but which also required the fewest apologies; which could be praised for their sobriety, prosperity, high educational level, good inns and roads; but which, alas, offered least in the way of adventure and exotic scenes and characters. A paean to American democratic society, the *Notions* is also an act of homage to Lafayette, whose triumphal tour of the United States in 1824 is recounted in some detail: Revolutionary war veterans embrace their former comrade-in-arms and tears flow; Mount Vernon and Monticello are piously revisited; a grateful Congress votes a gift of $200,000 and a section of land to pay off Lafayette's debts. As an expression of the fraternal spirit of international liberalism, the *Notions* is a touching if rather dull and misleading book. The account given of American political institutions, calculated to show that they are durable, dignified, and efficient, is remarkable only for its total complacency. Equally complacent is the account of contemporary party conflicts: Andrew Jackson is praised for his 'prudence' and 'indomitable resolution' and also for 'his usually mild and graceful mien'; but full of the spirit of the Era of Good Feeling, Cooper concludes impartially that 'men may well hesitate about rejecting so tried a patriot, and so experienced a statesman, as Mr [John Quincy] Adams'. 'The question', Cooper observes cheerfully, 'is altogether one of men, there being scarcely a measure of policy that is likely to be affected by the result.' No less reassuring is his description of the way public opinion arrives at the truth in a democratic society:

However agreeable habitual deference to forms may become, the pleasure is bought too dearly, when a just knowledge of ourselves, deceptive views of life, or even of sacred liberty itself, may be the price. I should cite America as furnishing the very reverse of this proposition. Here, without pretending to any infallibility of judgment, all matters are mooted with the most fearless indifference of the consequences. In the tossings and agitations of the public opinion, the fine and precious grains of truth gradually get winnowed from the chaff of empiricism and interestedness, and, to pursue the figure, literally become the mental aliment of the nation. After the mind is thoroughly imbued with the healthful moral truths, it admits the blandishments and exaggerations of conventional politeness with great distrust, and not unfrequently with distaste. . . . [The American] will not tell you he is enchanted to see you, when, in truth, he is perfectly indifferent to the matter; his thoughts are too direct for so gross a deception.

Here, in a very distant and fondly remembered America of 1827, is the perfect demoncratic 'candour' for which Cooper was to look in vain when, eleven year later, he wrote *The American Democrat*. The purpose of *Notions of the Americans* was to show how liberal theory worked out in practice, but the American republic described in it is a Fourth of July vision. This is not to suggest that America did not change (very much for the worse, in Cooper's judgement) between 1827 and 1838, but it is to insist that much of the change was in Cooper himself.

Inspired by the same liberal faith but more impressive both as literature and as political analysis is the novel, already referred to, which Cooper wrote during the aftermath of the July Revolution. *The Bravo* (1831) had the following history and aims:

Its outline was imagined during a short residence at Venice, several months previously to the occurrence of the late French revolution. I had had abundant occasion to observe that the great political contest of the age was not, as is usually pretended, between the two antagonist principles of monarchy and democracy, but in reality between the those who, under the shallow pretence of limiting power to the *élite* of society, were contending for exclusive advantages at the expense of the mass of their fellow-creatures. ...

I had it in view to exhibit the action of a narrow and exclusive system, by a simple and natural exposure of its influence on the familiar interests of life. The object was not to be attained by an essay, or a commentary, but by one of those popular pictures which find their way into every library; and which, whilst they have attractions for the feeblest intellects, are not often rejected by the strongest ... the object was to lay bare the wrongs that are endured by the weak, when the power is the exclusive property of the strong; the tendency of all exclusion to heartlessness; the irresponsible and ruthless movement of an aristocracy; the manner in which the selfish and wicked profit by its facilities; and in which even the good become the passive instruments of its soulless power. In short, I had undertaken to give the reader some idea of the action of a government, which to use the language of the book itself, had neither 'the high personal responsibility that sometimes tempers despotism by the qualities of the chief, nor the human impulses of popular rule.'

Such is the account given by Cooper in *A Letter to His Countrymen* (1834), a work which he wrote in reply to criticism levelled against him because of the revolutionary tendencies of *The Bravo* and his participation in the Finance Controversy. Clearly, the author of the *Notions* and *The Bravo* had moved a long way from the moderate conservatism of DeWitt Clinton and further still from the reactionary Federalism of his father. Clinton and William Cooper were American patriots of course, and so was James Cooper as much when he wrote *The Spy* as when he wrote the *Notions*. But there was a crucial difference between a patriot who created attractive pictures of life in America and an itinerant liberal who championed post-Jeffersonian American political principles even when his pictures were of Europe. Not surprisingly, conservative American editors who ap-

plauded the former were intensely suspicious of the latter.
Moreover, there was (and still is) some doubt as to the real
target of *The Bravo*. Old Venice was his ostensible subject,
but given his political associations he must have had contemporary Britain, France, and Russia in mind when he launched
this attack on aristocracy. Did he also have American upper-
class conservatives in view? The letters that have survived
from this period, while not so complacent as *Notions of
the Americans*, certainly do not suggest that he apprehended
any serious danger from that quarter. Jackson and his co-
horts might rumble darkly about the Second Bank of the
United States and its oligarchical supporters, but Cooper
appears to have been preoccupied – as well he might be –
with the actual revolutions that were going on around him
in Europe. Nevertheless, whatever his intentions, *The Bravo*
might easily be taken as an attack on the anti-Jackson forces.
And so it is scarcely surprising that the novel was denounced
by politically conservative editors and reviewers in America
as well as in France and England. To make matters worse,
both it and the *Notions* had comparatively poor sales in the
United States. Disappointed and frustrated, Cooper returned
home in 1833 convinced that the American 'reading classes',
i.e. the upper and middle classes, were out of sympathy with
his democratic principles. A year later, in *A Letter to His
Countrymen*, he became an open enemy of the Whig, or,
as he now saw it, the oligarchical party in the United States.

Whether *The Bravo* was partly aimed at American conservatives is a question worth pursuing somewhat further.
It was in 1830, before writing *The Bravo*, that Cooper first
declared himself a convert to Jefferson's ideas: 'Have we not
had a false idea of that man? I own he begins to appear to
me, to be the greatest man, we ever had'. He adds: 'His
knowledge of Europe was of immense service to him. Without it, no American is fit to speak of the institutions of his
own Country'*. As a close student of Jefferson's writings at

Letters, I, 411.

23

this time, he might well have come across the following passage in *Notes on the State of Virginia**, in which Jefferson criticizes the Virginian Constitution:

All the powers of government, legislative, executive, and judiciary, result to the legislative body. The concentrating these in the same hands is precisely the definition of despotic government. It will be no alleviation that these powers will be exercised by a plurality of hands, and not by a single one. 173 despots would surely be as oppressive as one. Let those who doubt it turn their eyes on the republic of Venice.

Perhaps, following up his hint from Jefferson, Cooper did mean his American readers to 'turn their eyes on the republic of Venice' and be warned. But we cannot be sure. Venice was frequently used by liberals and radicals as a particularly appalling example of oligarchical despotism; Lord Byron's *Marino Faliero* (1821), for instance, is a Venetian political tragedy very like *The Bravo* and is actually quoted in Cooper's novel. Byron, Jefferson, or a dozen other writers might have suggested the possibilities of Venice as a subject for political fiction, and to the student of politics it doesn't matter greatly whether any of them did. What does matter in this context is that Jefferson uses Venice as an example of an 'elective despotism' brought about when one branch of government, the legislative, usurps the powers of the executive and judicial branches. In *The Bravo*, Cooper's well-intentioned Doge, the nominal executive head of state, is unable to prevent the ruthless acts of the Venetian Senate. In *A Letter to His Countrymen* and *The American Democrat*, one of the chief dangers to American democracy is diagnosed as 'legislative usurpation', i.e. attempts by Congress to take over functions which are the prerogative of the President. Now in all these cases Cooper's analysis is based on principles derived from Locke and Montesquieu and built into the American Constitution by

*XII, 4.

their American disciples. However, by adapting these principles to a profoundly democratic ethos, Cooper makes them distinctively Jeffersonian.

Jeffersonian too was the social-political stance Cooper now assumed. Wealth, social position, education, and talent all marked Jefferson out as an 'American aristocrat', but he had made himself the champion of the masses. Jefferson's and Cooper's own friend Lafayette was an authentic aristocrat, but for half a century he had risked his life and fortune for the sake of popular rights. Neither felt that there was any necessary conflict between the quiet enjoyment of his social privileges and his active campaign for political rights for all. Cooper made their position his own, and at the same time recognized that this would not recommend him to his social peers:

With us the *people* are national, from affection, and a consciousness of living under a system that protects their rights and interests. But true nationality is very much confined to the mass, though national conceit is pretty generally diffused. No man in America can have national pride ... who has not pride in the institutions; and this is a feeling that all the training of the higher classes has taught them to repress.*

During this period, Cooper admitted that American democracy was vulnerable to demagoguery and levelling tendencies. Both of these dangers are illustrated in his tedious Swiftian political allegory *The Monikins* (1835). But generally he minimized their importance and argued that the social aristocracy had nothing to fear from the mass:

Jefferson was the man to whom we owe the high lesson that the *natural* privileges of a social aristocracy are in truth no more than their *natural* privileges. With us, all questions of personal rights, except those of the poor slaves, are effectually settled, and yet every valuable interest is as secure as it is anywhere else.†

* *Gleanings in Europe: England.*
† *Letters*, II, 180.

Indeed, he went so far as to say that 'every hour I stay at home, convinces me more and more, that society has had a summerset, and that the élite is at the bottom!'* Ridiculing the fears of the middle classes in *A Letter to His Countrymen*, he boasts of himself: 'I had not been cooped up in a ward of New-York, regarding things only on one side, and working myself into a fever on the subject of the imminent danger that impended over this great republic, by the machinations of a few "working-men", dreaming of agrarian laws. ...' Which is perfectly true: he had spent seven years abroad developing a lofty detachment from the fears natural to his own class, and a warm sympathy for the lower classes that in Europe were, and in America might be, deprived of their political rights. This perspective on American politics was a noble, exhilarating one – and would remain unobscured just so long as the working-man resisted the oratory of the Whig demagogues and carried on merely 'dreaming of agrarian laws'.

Had *The American Democrat* been written from this perspective, it would have been very different from the book we actually have. In fact, it was written after the first of a series of social and political shocks which left Cooper, at the end of his life, thoroughly disillusioned with American democracy. Coming as it does at a transitional point in the development of his political thought, *The American Democrat* has neither the sweet liberalism of *Notions of the Americans* nor the sour conservatism of his last work, but a special pungent flavour of its own. To understand the transitional nature of the book, we shall have to review his later work in relation to the events that finally drove him back into the conservative camp.

The first of these events seems petty enough today, but it hurt Cooper personally and ended by involving him in litigation and making him the victim of a national scandal. In 1836, after a long residence in New York City and several

Letters, III, 42.

European capitals, the Cooper family at last returned to Cooperstown, where after refurbishing William Cooper's old manor house in the latest neo-gothick style they commenced uneasy relations with their bucolic neighbours. Politics and outdoor sports seem to have been the chief pastimes of the villagers, who were just then busy inventing baseball and supporting two local, rival party newspapers. Another popular recreation was picnicking on Three Mile Point, a scenic little projection into Lake Otsego belonging to the Cooper family but commonly supposed to be public property. Repeated depredations at the Point led Cooper in 1837 to issue a mild warning which, when loudly resented and denounced at a large public meeting, was abruptly transformed into a NO TRESPASSING injunction. He believed that a majority of those who denounced him and his title to the Point (and also demanded that copies of his books in the village library be publicly burned) were presumptuous newcomers to Cooperstown, who of all people were least qualified, but most ready, to decide questions of local usages and rights. Trivial, unfortunate, foolish on both sides, the incident was seized on by the Whig press and magnified into an unfeeling act of tyranny by an 'Aristo' who also happened to be one of the state's best known supporters of 'King Andrew' and 'Crown Prince' Martin Van Buren. The whole affair would doubtless have been quickly forgotten had the sensitive novelist held his peace. But accepting the enemy's valuation of its importance Cooper decided that the 'lessons' of the Three Mile Point affair should be stated as bluntly and published as widely as possible.

What were these lessons? First in importance, perhaps, was that there was a dangerous assumption current in America that the convenience of the public took precedence over the rights of the private individual. Second, that deference to public opinion ('They say') and uncritical acceptance of rumour in the form of gossip or newspaper reports were

becoming habits which threatened the basis of any enlightened democratic action. Third, that political party
hostilities had become as fierce and destructive of truth
(especially in the newspapers) as ever they were during the evil
days of Federalist-Republican rivalry. And fourth, that the
migratory habits of Americans began to menace American
civilization by assuring that they would tend to look out for
themselves rather than for the community, and in any
case would be too ill-informed about local facts and issues
to know what really was in the community's best interests.

These lessons were hammered home not only in *The
American Democrat* but also in several other books published in 1838 which were mainly or partly inspired by the
Three Mile Point affair: a history of his native village
entitled *The Chronicles of Cooperstown*, and a pair of novels,
Homeward Bound and *Home as Found*, which presents a
thinly fictionalized (but richly biased) version of the Cooper
family's tribulations in America. *The American Democrat*
has other, more national and theoretical bones to pick as
well. Cooper was so deeply interested in the major controversies of the Jacksonian period – Nullification, Internal
Improvements, the Bank War – that he would probably
have written a work like *The American Democrat* even
without the provocation of the Three Mile Point episode.
Washington, D.C., not Cooperstown, N.Y., was the village
his mind inhabited, and he was more familiar with its
characters, its institutions, and its vagaries than with those
of his home town. Nevertheless, he knew that American
democracy depended as much on local attitudes, population
densities, and communications media as it did on federal
governmental machinery and constitutional construction.
He believed that the United States government was the
best yet devised by man, and he was very ready to join
Lafayette in spreading the liberal gospel. But he also believed, with Jefferson, that some nations were not yet fit
for the American system – and that those that were might

grow unfit for it. Hence, in part, his preoccupation with concrete local matters. At the same time, Cooper was a novelist as well as a political thinker, and it was these concrete local matters which lent themselves especially well to fictional treatment. And since it was as a novelist that he was taken most seriously and most widely read by his contemporaries, *Home as Found* rather than *The American Democrat* was the book that created a sensation in 1838 and goaded his Whig enemies into editorial retaliation – retaliation which forced him in turn to identify his interests more closely with those of two superficially contradictory groups, the landed gentry and the party of Andrew Jackson.

The story of an expatriate American family (the 'Effinghams') coming home to New York and Cooperstown ('Templeton'), with harsh and detailed accounts of urban and rural American society, *Home as Found* contains among other things a highly coloured version of the Three Mile Point affair, a favourable reference to President Jackson, an apocalyptic vision of Wall Street going up in retributive flames, and a slashing attack on several types of Whigs. Of these Whigs, the most sympathetically drawn is wealthy, urban-based John Effingham, a man of character and intelligence but of loose attachment to the *patria* and almost no sympathy with American democracy. This character can probably be taken as a fairly accurate generalized portrait of many of Cooper's upper-class New York City Whig friends: the oligarchical party at its best, moderated in this case by the benign influence of the landed gentry as represented by cousin Edward Effingham, Squire of Templeton. Least sympathetically portrayed is one Steadfast Dodge, a cowardly obsequious newspaper editor who is a willing slave to public opinion and a ready traducer of personal reputations. This caricature, which belongs as much to the world of the nineteenth-century political cartoons as to that of literature, was patently designed to infuriate the Whig press.

But although Cooper was ferocious in his frontal assaults, he gave little thought to defensive strategies: the autobiographical sections of *Home as Found* left him wide open to a Whig counter-attack. Squire Edward Effingham, clearly intended to be a somewhat bland Jeffersonian figure, could be ridiculed as an infatuated self-portrait and solid proof that Cooper's European experience had transformed him into a mindless aristophile. Just the opposite was true, but the very palpable truth did not prevent a leading Whig editor from accusing Cooper of

aristocratical pretensions; and publishing a book to demonstrate that he is a scion of a noble English family living on 'the estate of his father', in a kind of baronial style, consonant alike with the early education, noble descent, and habitual tastes of the 'mild and thoughtful Mr Effingham', whose 'well regulated mind', had pointed out to him the moral grandeur of such a man gradually descending into the vale of years surrounded by a dependent peasantry. ...

This travesties Cooper's position, but it is typical of attacks made on him and other leading Democrats by Whig editors who, by 1838, were actively reversing the charismatic image of the Jacksonian party as a party of the People, a party locked in moral combat with an evil oligarchical party (i.e. the Whigs). The 'aristocratic Mr Effingham' became a national target of Whig abuse – less scurrilous abuse than that heaped on the 'crown' of President Van Buren, but surely much more painful to the novelist than to the politician. Cooper countered with a series of libel suits which, though more than nominally successful, left him scarcely better off than the deposed Van Buren; for the Whig newspapers stopped their libels of the man but also stopped their reviews of his books.

Already shaken by the Three Mile Point incident, Cooper's late-developed faith in democracy could not stand up under the series of blows it was dealt soon thereafter.

The election of General Harrison on a platform of log cabins and hard cider seemed to demonstrate the vulnerability of the electorate to demagoguery and campaign stunts. And certainly the successful Whig campaign against 'aristocracy' was as cynical as it was crude – so far as party managers like Boss Thurlow Weed were concerned. Worse – in Cooper's eyes – the feeling it aroused among American voters was quite genuine, and that feeling could be turned against real targets as well as phantom aristocrats. Moreover, in New York Governor William Henry Seward and *New York Tribune* editor Horace Greeley, the Whig party had leaders with authentic (if intermittent) radical impulses who could exploit and partially control the situation. Cooper now discovered that working-men were not merely 'dreaming of agrarian laws'. In 1839 and for several years afterwards, tenants on the great New York estates owned by Cooper's friends agitated with considerable success for the reform of leases and the gradual dissolution of the estates themselves. Governor Seward openly sympathized with this assault on the rights of property; Cooper wrote a trilogy of novels (*Satanstoe, The Chainbearer,* and *The Redskins*) defending the landlords and insisting on their constitutional rights. Greeley published a series of articles advocating Fourierist experiments; Cooper retaliated with an anti-utopia (*The Crater*) which not only attacked socialist principles but even predicted the demise of the American republic as a result of demagogues' and newspapers' inciting the populace to violate the Constitution. Reforms of the legal system, notably the institution of an elective judiciary, provoked Cooper in his last novel, *The Ways of the Hour* (1850), to show how a democratized system of elected judge and jury could subvert justice.

In his last, unfinished work, a history of New York City, Cooper came full circle politically. To all the other symptoms of national disintegration were added the rival agitations of abolitionists and secessionists, both of whom Cooper heartily detested. So far as he could see, 'the future of this country holds out but three possible solutions to the tendencies of the present time – viz. the bayonet, a return to the true principles of the original government, or the sway of money'. The last – oligarchy ruling through the forms of democracy – now seemed the most likely solution. And although he continued to deplore the corrupting effects of wealth, he feared anarchy and Caesarism more than an urban-based oligarchy: agrarian riots had dispersed the old Jeffersonian myth of the virtuous husbandman, and it was apparent that the country gentry needed all the help it could get from town money. For the material progress of the country he had no fears, but he died in 1851 believing that the American political experiment had pretty well failed.

Both chronologically and ideologically *The American Democrat* stands equidistant from the blithely optimistic *Notions of the Americans* and the grimly pessimistic *Towns of Manhattan*. It is the work of a badly shaken but still convinced liberal, whose unfavourable impressions of European political systems are still fresh, but who has had very recent and unnerving personal experience in America of the party press, exaltation of public opinion, migratory habits, crudity of manners and language, lack of respect for privacy, lack of frankness, casual attention to property rights, levelling tendencies generally, etc. etc. Some of his complaints are petty and snobbish – grievances of an unappreciated Enlightener in the midst of provincial darkness. Yet we shall fail to understand *The American Democrat* if we fail to see that, for Cooper as for many of his contemporaries, American democracy was still a great social and political experiment that had to prove itself by the quality of daily life it engendered: it might win its wars with the English and Indians, it might boast about abolishing the feudal evils of hereditary titles and an established religion, but did it safeguard property and make possible the civilization – arts, manners, privacy – which made life tolerable to men like Cooper himself? If he demanded much for his class in terms of the quality of local daily life, he also believed that a citizen of that class should act locally to improve that quality and be a 'guardian of the liberties of his fellow citizens' of all classes. *The American Democrat* is such an act. It was first published, not by one of the major firms of Philadelphia or London that handled his novels, but by a local Cooperstown press. It was evidently designed to be used as a textbook in the New York state school system. This grassroots approach helps account for the format of the book – brief pithy lessons – and the stress on mundane duties – social as well as political – of the ordinary citizen. Given its intended local function, it might seem strange that *The American Democrat* does not refer directly to contemporary local issues. But Cooper believed that the business of education was to inculcate permanently valid general principles which, once mastered, would enable students to judge particular issues for themselves. For the same reason, he does not directly discuss the great party political issues of the Jacksonian era: the implicit argument of *The American Democrat* is that these issues would not even exist if Americans really understood their own political principles. Today serious students of Cooper's political thought must infer from his principles what issues he had in mind. But the permanent interest and readability of the book are doubtless due to his focus on the general and enduring aspects of American political life.

THE JACKSONIAN CONTEXT

Throughout his career, Cooper reaffirmed the Founding Fathers' view that political parties were a great evil. His incantatory denunciation of party in *The American Democrat* is delivered with the passion and moral certitude of a priest expounding sacred texts:

When party rules, the people do not rule, but merely such a portion of the people as can manage to get the control of party. . . .

It is a very different thing to be a democrat, and to be a member of what is called a democratic party; for the first insists on his independence and an entire freedom of opinion, while the last is incompatible with either.

Here is an unambiguous declaration of independence by a highly individualistic man; Cooper was unquestionably sincere when he made it; and yet, as we have seen, he was frequently attacked and victimized as a leading spokesman for the Democratic party. Moreover, it can be shown that *The American Democrat* takes a fairly consistent Jacksonian line. Was Cooper a party man or not? Rather than 'a member of what is called a democratic party', perhaps it would be better to say that he was a Jeffersonian and a staunch anti-Whig: his enthusiasm for Jackson and Van Buren as politicians was sharply qualified, but his hostility to Clay, Webster, and Seward was not: he did indeed agree with Jackson on many points of principle, but the libellous attacks on himself by the Whig press made him regard Jackson's opponents as men of no principle at all. The matter is further complicated by the fact that neither Cooper nor the Whigs stood still ideologically during the 1830s. It became increasingly difficult to tell who was 'Jacksonian' and who was not. Early in the decade, as a coalition of anti-Jackson elements forced by Jackson to establish an identity by rallying around the U.S. Bank, the Whigs could be plausibly attacked as the 'oligarchical' party by a then very liberal James Fenimore Cooper. Later in the decade, with the rise of Thurlow Weed as party manager and the emergence of Harrison as a 'People's' presidential candidate, the political style of the Whigs became 'Jacksonian'; while in practice as in propaganda many Whig politicians, particularly Seward, became more zealous about popular rights than the now majority-shy novelist. Nonetheless – in the

Free States – the Whig party remained the 'oligarchical party' in so far as there was one: its great conservative theoretician Daniel Webster continued to defend the interests of State and Wall Streets, and continued to have his retainer 'freshened' by the U.S. Bank; a generous portion of the funds that elected Seward and Harrison were donated by the 'merchant prince' clients of Thurlow Weed. And in spite of his reactionary drift, the author of *The American Democrat* was still a Jacksonian, though only a small-*d* democrat.

The heart of Cooper's Jacksonianism – indeed, the heart of the political philosophy of *The American Democrat* – is probably to be found in the section 'On Property'. Possibly he would have agreed with Jefferson that Locke's natural rights of Life, Liberty, and Property should be rephrased as 'Life, Liberty, and the Pursuit of Happiness'. At any rate, when he writes that 'we may infer that the rights of property, to a certain extent, are founded in nature', the qualifying phrase 'to a certain extent' does weaken the force of his inference slightly. But only slightly. No more than Locke, the Founding Fathers (Jefferson included), or Andrew Jackson does Cooper doubt the absolute necessity of defending property. He was familiar with the theories of Saint-Simon, Fourier, and Robert Owen; but he was also familiar with the 'failure of all attempts to form communities, even on a small scale, with a common interest'. He was sure he knew why they failed:

The principle of individuality, or to use a less winning term, of selfishness, lies at the root of all voluntary human exertion. We toil for food, for clothes, for houses, lands, and for property, in general. This is done, because we know that the fruits of our labor will belong to ourselves, or to those who are most dear to us. It follows, that all which society enjoys beyond the mere supply of its first necessities, is dependant on the rights of property.

35

Such was the view not only of Cooper but of Webster and James Kent, not only of Jefferson but of Hamilton and John Adams. Where he differed essentially from the leading Federalists and conservative Whigs was in his conviction that property should not control government through special representation. To their argument that men of property were the ones with a stake in society and should therefore govern it, he replied:

Every man who has wants, feelings, affections and character, has a stake in society. Of the two, perhaps, the necessities of men are a greater corrective of political abuses, than their surplus means. Both may lead to evil, beyond a doubt, but, as laws which are framed by all, must be tolerably impartial and general in their operation, less danger arises from the rule of the former, than from the rule of the latter.... Property always carries with it a portion of indirect political influence, and it is unwise, and even dangerous, to strengthen this influence by adding to it constitutional privileges; the result always being to make the strong stronger, and the weak weaker.

Cooper's message is the Jacksonian message: not the whole of it, of course, but the most fundamental part.

In his discussions of property in *The American Democrat* there is always a powerful tension, verging on contradiction, between his absolute commitment to the defence of property and his conviction that it ought not to rule. Most members of his class, concerned as he was about potential encroachments on property rights, would have concluded that the tension was intolerable, that to be safe property needed institutionalized power to defend itself. But in politics as in literature, Cooper's mind revelled in such unresolved tensions, and his analysis of most ethical or political problems tended to be governed by the premises that, in the case of every great good, 'its abuses are in proportion to its benefits' and that the 'tendency of man ... [is] to convert into curses things that Providence designed to prove benefits'. Thus, 'property is an instrument of working most of the good that society enjoys'; but at the same time, 'property [is] an influence the most corrupting to which men submit, and which, when its ordinary temptations are found united to those of political patronage and power, is much too strong for human virtue'. Ambivalent this is, but not confused or imprecise. The same qualities characterize his discussions of the press, liberty, self-government, and other subjects in *The American Democrat*. Clearly, a mind that works in this way is likely to be in sympathy with a system of government based on an elaborate division and balance of powers – a system which, working as it does through complex tensions, is a kind of analogue of that mind. The consequence of all these factors is that Cooper's understanding of American politics is more subtle and complicated than one might expect of a man of his social class and simple, strict moral code.

This combination of complicated understanding and simple Christian morality made him a reluctant Jacksonian but a poor party man. Mankind as a whole he considered half animal, half divine – a view which cut across class lines and prevented whole-hearted party affiliation. Unlike the more radical Democrats – young Walt Whitman, for example – he had little faith in the moral purity and instinctive political wisdom of the masses. Unlike the more reactionary Whigs – James Kent, for instance – he could not divide mankind into 'the industrious and virtuous' on the one hand, and 'the indolent and profligate' on the other. Men of all classes being what they were, they needed to be governed; but being what they were, neither the rich nor the poor, neither the minority nor the majority could be expected to govern very well. He therefore favoured that form of government which had strictly limited powers, which offered exclusive privileges to none, and which held the executive, legislative, and judicial powers in balance. He favoured strict construction of the Constitution. These, precisely, were the doctrines which Cooper and Jackson had inherited from Jefferson; and, like Jackson, Cooper originally adopted them because he then – during the 1820s – shared Jefferson's optimistic view of 'the People'. Now the same doctrines were justified by a very different view:

No expedients can equalize the temporal lots of man; for without civilization and government, the strong would oppress the weak, and, with them, an inducement to exertion must be left, by bestowing rewards on talents, industry and success. All that the best institutions, then, can achieve, is to remove useless obstacles, and to permit merit to be the artisan of its own fortune, without always degrading demerit to the place it ought naturally to fill.

This is virtually to build a Jeffersonian superstructure on a Hobbesian base. This seems incongrous, but it meant that, more clearly than other leading Jacksonians, Cooper perceived the nightmarish shadows which lurked in the freely competitive society of Jefferson's and Jackson's dreams.

Many of the major controversies of the Jackson and Van Buren administrations are alluded to or discussed indirectly in more or less detail in the pages of *The American Democrat*. Its opening sections are especially rich in analyses of the various constitutional issues raised by Nullification and the Bank War. Cooper discussed these issues not in order to influence the outcome – already decided – of the controversies themselves, but in order to clarify important principles which had been obscured and distorted by sectional or party squabbling. This is not to suggest that the issues were dead or merely academic: Jacksonian majorities had won the day, but the issues might, and did, crop up again to disturb the peace of the Republic.

As a strict constructionist, Cooper insisted in *The American Democrat* that the federal government was a government of explicitly limited powers, all the powers of government not enumerated in the Constitution being reserved to the states. Moreover, he agreed with Jefferson and the chief theoretician of Nullification, Calhoun, that the sovereign states acting individually – not the people of all the states acting together – had formed the Constitution and, in so doing, ceded to the federal government what powers it had. Working from this premiss, Calhoun had argued that a state, still sovereign, might act unilaterally to nullify – declare unconstitutional and inoperative within its own boundaries – a law passed regularly by the Congress and President, and declared constitutional by the U.S. Supreme Court. When Calhoun's South Carolina did just this in 1832, in response to a tariff which seemed to favour northern industrial states at the expense of the agricultural south, Jackson replied to the Nullifiers' reasoning that they had got their premiss wrong: the people as a whole had created the Constitution, thus forming a Union which was not a league of sovereign states but a nation. Jackson won this battle, not with words, but with a crafty policy which combined threatened force with substantial concessions. But the issue was a crucial one which needed to be aired and, if possible, settled once and for all without resort to arms. Cooper tried to meet the problem, which was at bottom a sectional economic and social problem involving slavery, by arguing (in 'On Representation') that federal legislators ought to represent the interests of the entire nation and not merely those of their local constituencies, since 'the union of these states is founded on an express compromise, and it is not its intention to reach a benefit, however considerable, by extorting undue sacrifices from particular members of the confederacy.' At the same time, he insisted (in 'On the Republick of the United States of America') that the states by ratifying the federal Constitution had virtually ceased to be sovereign:

... too much importance is attached to what is called the reserved sovereignties of the several states. A community can hardly be termed sovereign at all, which has parted with all the great powers of sovereignty, such as the control of foreign relations, the authority to make war and peace, to regulate commerce, to coin money, keep fleets and armies, with all the other powers that have been ceded by the states to the federal government. But, admitting that the rights reserved are sovereign in their ordinary nature, they are scarcely so in the conditions under which they are enjoyed, since, by an amendment of the constitution, a state may be deprived of most of them, without its own consent.

Whereas Calhoun's reading of the Constitution left the federal government at the mercy of individual states, Cooper's reading does exactly the opposite. In his view, the federal Constitution was indeed the Supreme Law of the Land. True, he recognized that where an individual state's interests were identified with broad sectional interests (as in the case of slavery), states' rights would not in fact be whittled away by constitutional amendment; he was also firm in insisting that the Supreme Court 'cannot make the constitution, in any case; it only interprets the law'. But amendments *could* be made; and in the case of powers already constitutionally ceded to the federal government, such as the power of regulating tariffs, individual states or minority sections could only hope that the majority would act in the idealistic spirit recommended by Cooper. An unrealistic hope, it might seem, but the remarkable thing is that on the whole the majority did so act: it was the fantastic southern secessionists, losing faith in the system, who acted 'realistically'.

Though the issues revitalized by the Nullification controversy were to prove more important in the long run, the various problems of constitutional interpretation raised by the Bank War were scarcely less fundamental. The Bank War tended to divide the nation not only along sectional lines but along class and party lines as well. The violent feelings thus inspired did for a time cause both Congress and President to play fast and loose with the Constitution in a truly alarming way.

Whatever its actual merits, Jackson saw the Second Bank of the United States as 'the Monster': an oligarchical institution which favoured north-eastern financial interests at the expense of the rest of the nation; a great federally chartered private corporation which, as the exclusive depository of federal funds, had sufficient capital and centralized power to manipulate the economy of the entire nation. The old General was suspicious of all banks, and this was the Bank of Banks. Though the Supreme Court decision of *McCulloch v. Maryland* had recognized the constitutional power of the federal government to establish such corporations, Jackson, no admirer of former Chief Justice Marshall or his Federalist policies, was prepared to use his veto power to express his judgement to the contrary. He did so in 1832 when the Bank sought a new charter, and soon thereafter, though the Bank's present charter had several years to run, he ordered Secretary of the Treasury Duane to begin removing federal deposits from the Bank. Duane refused, Duane was fired. Meanwhile, the powerful anti-Jackson coalition of Senators Clay, Webster, and Calhoun fought back vehemently: denouncing Old Hickory's high-handed dismissal of previous Supreme Court decisions; crying that his use of the veto power was irresponsible and dictatorial and in violation of the spirit of the Constitution; and at last blocking the President's nominations and passing a resolution censuring him for his dismissal of Duane. The practical consequences of the Bank War were that Jackson gained even greater popularity with the public, and that the nation lost the one institution capable of keeping its currency stable.

Writing after the Depression of 1837, Cooper was privately reconsidering the merits of 'the Monster'. Perhaps second thoughts about the Bank, as well as his general policy of avoiding direct references to contemporary issues, prevented him from making emphatic pronouncements on the constitutionality of such an institution in *The American Democrat*. However, his championship of 'hard money' ('On the Circulating Medium') was typical of those Democrats who attacked the Bank as the leading issuer of paper notes. And his discussion of the relationship between commerce and the federal government ('On Commerce'), though somewhat vague, was strict constructionist in tenor and by implication opposed to the Hamiltonian-Whig case for the Bank:

All legislation affecting the currency, commerce and banking, in a country like this, ought to be limited, as far as circumstances will allow, to general and simple provisions, the nature of the institutions forbidding the interference that is elsewhere practised with advantage.... It follows, that the interference of the government with all such questions, in this country, should be unfrequent and cautious, since it possesses a power to injure, with very little power to benefit.

What concerned Cooper much more than the constitutionality of the Bank was the constitutionality of the various actions taken by the President and the Senate during the War – actions which directly involved the division and balance of powers in the government. In the first place ('On Distinctive American Principles'), he defended the right of the President to veto a law on constitutional grounds even though the Supreme Court had pronounced similar measures constitutional, and even though in doing so the executive was temporarily assuming legislative and judicial functions. In the last resort, after all, Congress retained the legislative power and the courts the judicial power, since Congress could override the veto and the President could not execute a law declared unconstitutional by the Supreme Court. Cooper's case for permitting the President to veto a law on constitutional grounds in spite of previous court decisions is not argued very fully or clearly; but his belief seems to have been that if the President and Congress were barred from passing or vetoing new laws because of existing court decisions, the court would in effect be making rather than – as was intended – merely interpreting the laws. Besides, the modification and inquiry desirable in changing circumstances, and encouraged by the balance of powers, would be seriously inhibited.

Cooper was much more explicit and detailed in his commentary on the relations between the President and Congress, devoting most of two relatively long sections ('On Distinctive American Principles' and 'On the Powers of the Executive') to a major analysis of the respective powers of the executive and legislative branches. His argument is complex and at the same time is so cogently made as not to require summary here, but if one reads between the lines one can see that it is a passionate defence of President Jackson. Cooper ridicules (always by implication) the Whig claims that Jackson's use of the veto amounted to a tyranny of the executive branch: following the *Federalist* interpretation that the presidential veto power is a necessary check on the most powerful and least responsible branch of the government, he turns the tables by arguing that the Whig Senators' recent actions amounted to a most unconstitutional and un-American attempt to establish legislative tyranny. In particular, he defends the President's (Jackson's) right and duty to remove officers (Secretary of Treasury Duane) who fail to carry out his orders, denying that the Senate has any right to interfere with, to debate about, or to pass resolutions censuring the President in matters involving the executive prerogative. To say that Cooper's argument is a complete vindication of the old chieftain of the Democratic party is in no way to suggest that it was veiled propaganda for that party. Cooper did indeed believe that anglophile Whig leaders like Webster wished by legislative usurpation to pervert the American system into the oligarchical parliamentary system of Britain, but the analysis offered here is an elaboration of principles stated by Cooper several years before the Bank War and the birth of the Whig party. Basically, it is no more than a systematic re-affirmation of the need for strict observance of the separation and balance of powers: Jackson is vindicated because, as Cooper saw it, he resisted all attempts to trespass on the powers and upset their balance.

Though anti-, or perhaps it would be truer to say, post-Jacksonian in its preoccupation with minority rather than majority rights, *The American Democrat* deviates surprisingly little from the Democratic party position on specific contemporary issues. Perhaps the chief heresy is Cooper's repudiation of *laissez-faire* economics, which were endorsed by both Jefferson and Jackson as an essential feature of their free, minimally governed society. Though desiring as little governmental intervention as possible in commercial affairs, Cooper was sure that American Free Traders were the dupes of English doctrines and propaganda ('On Publick Opinion'). His reasoning was simple, sound, and thoroughly Hamiltonian: when the United States equalled or surpassed Britain as an industrial nation, then it too should advocate Free Trade. On most other points of national policy, Hamilton and his Whig heirs had few more adamant and perceptive opponents than this son of arch-Federalist William Cooper. He knew them well, and he was getting to know the followers of Jackson pretty well, too.

THE MODERN CONTEXT

The American Democrat is undoubtedly of interest to anyone seeking to understand the period in which it was written. The question remains whether the work has any relevance to our own times. It has been shown that the book contains clear, if indirect, references to major issues of the Age of Jackson. Since many of those issues have now been settled, one might well wonder if it is possible to consider Cooper's observations appropriate to the circumstances of the twentieth century. The perspicacity of de Tocqueville's discussion of American democracy has lent his work great durability. Can Cooper be placed in the same class?

It must be admitted that Cooper lacked the originality of Tocqueville and that he failed to develop his ideas as thoroughly; yet he has much the same type of contemporary interest. Both men are meaningful to the present generation because of the types of problems they considered. Men in every age write about the problems which disturb them, and venting of political feeling with varying degrees of acrimony is characteristic of all times, even when ideas must be disguised in order to avoid censorship. Regardless of their immediate impact, however, most such works are important, if at all, merely for a brief period. They serve their purpose and then disappear. Only a few are read by succeeding generations. The difference is essentially that between political theory and polemic. Cooper, of course, made no claim to either category; he was writing primarily to correct error and to clarify. Yet his work is more than a tract for his times. Although frequently drawn to Jacksonian politics, he genuinely disliked political party activity and could accurately claim to be independent of narrow partisan interest. The problems he considered, rather, were those transcending particular times or particular events in history. Questions of a National Bank or of Nullification are of only ephemeral interest, however important at the time, but there are larger issues behind them. It was to the latter that Cooper most often directed his attention. The Bank issue would eventually be resolved, but problems of congressional power continually demand attention; the Nullification controversy has been permanently settled, but problems of definition in a federal system remain.

Primarily, then, because of his insight, his ability to distinguish the perennial problems of political man from the merely transitory, Cooper has stood the test of time. It is possible to recognize the contemporary issues to which he referred, but they are subsidiary to his main purpose, which was to consider questions arising out of a democratic America. Those questions, of course, are basically those which have aroused the interest of most intellectuals concerned with the nature of political control. Thus, there are portions of the book reminiscent of Aristotle and Locke, as well as of the writers of *The Federalist*. In most instances, the questions have no final answers, and it is for that reason that men of each generation must try to discover the manner in which their particular age shall seek to handle them. It is for that reason also that the questions never lose their interest or their challenge.

Some of Cooper's ideas, it is true, seem a bit outmoded when judged from the vantage point of the twentieth century. His rather frequent references to natural and divine law were perfectly in harmony with prevailing ideas, but the destructiveness of two world wars and changing ideas on the nature of man have considerably weakened faith in natural justice. His belief that American opinion tends to be dominated by foreign influences seems especially obsolete today after a period of American isolationism and parochialism, followed by attempts to spread the American 'way of life' through as much of the world as possible. His notions that right ultimately triumphs and that truth will always prevail (which probably owe much to Milton) have lost a great deal of meaning because of the growth of mass propaganda and increasingly effective means of totalitarian control. His ideas on the press are sometimes limited by the anger of personal experience.

In a few places, changes since 1838 make Cooper's ideas seem more than usually dated. Most readers will probably be a bit amused by his discussion of manners, the duties of private station, and of language. Even in those parts, however, Cooper's remarks are not without a degree of validity today. Although his discussion of language, for example, is decidedly pedantic, it does indirectly at least point to an interesting relationship between the American language and the American character. It is fascinating to note how closely related are language and notions of equality. In Britain, for example, accent is one of the major means of indicating social status. With notable exceptions, there is a distinct relationship between a person's position in society and the manner in which he speaks. Conscious efforts are made to change or improve accents, and there is still an interest in the 'well-spoken' person. Although one might well quarrel with the motives, the result has been a minority which has in some way been concerned with maintaining a sensitivity to the various nuances and graces available in the English language.

In America, on the other hand, nearly the reverse has been true. Equality has seemed to lead to the idea that one person should speak very much like another. There are regional variations it is true, but aside from those there is very little difference. Rather than a minority seeking to maintain standards of spoken American, there is instead acceptance of majority usage at nearly all levels of society. Sameness is considered desirable, for no one wants to be thought affected or accused of 'putting on airs'. Thus language tends to have been levelled downwards; businessmen, college professors, and upper-class governors speak much the same as dustmen.

It is when Cooper discusses the separation of powers that his analysis seems most irrelevant to this century. That was a notion to which Cooper was very keenly committed, for, like Montesquieu, he regarded the concentration of power in a single place to be the essence of tyranny. He felt, therefore, that one of the major virtues of the American system of government was the way in which governing powers had been divided between the legislative and executive branches, and he was concerned to maintain the balance. Accordingly, he devoted quite a number of pages to his belief that the Congress threatened to usurp all power and to dominate the country completely. It is not difficult, looking at that period, to see why such fears arose, and of course Cooper was not alone in holding such views. In fact, the threat of congressional control continued for some time, and fifty years later Woodrow Wilson felt it necessary to reiterate the warning. But in the second half of the twentieth century, when executive domination has become the norm in virtually all societies and when efforts are being made to resuscitate legislatures, Cooper's words seem hardly more than historical curiosities.

Cooper's fear of legislative domination led him also to miscalculate the role which the presidency was to play in American government. Fear of a strong executive had been very strong in America at the time of the War of Independence; to ensure adoption of the Constitution, the authors of *The Federalist* found it necessary to assure the nation that the President would bear no resemblance to the British monarch and that his powers would be strictly limited. Cooper felt that the limitations had indeed been too effective and threatened to negate the principle of balance of powers. The danger to the Republic was not the power of the President, but rather his ineffectiveness. Even today there are some who would argue that the President is not provided with sufficient power to deal with problems he must face; in general, however, commentators agree that there has been a marked and apparently irreversible shift in the other direction.

The surprising thing about Cooper, however, is not that he was wrong when weighing the respective powers of Congress and the President; it is, rather, that so many of his observations are still meaningful. Writers for centuries have discussed the dangers to democracy from unfettered majority rule, but Cooper renews the discussion and adapts it to peculiarly American conditions. Again, although his bias against political parties is especially acute, he nonetheless manages to express in very relevant terms what parties can mean in a system like the American. And his discussion of representation is very modern in outlook, despite or because of its Burkean overtones. But the acuteness of Cooper's observations can be seen perhaps most vividly in his comments on slavery. Although unsympathetic to slavery, Cooper was not adamantly opposed to it on moral or religious grounds; he believed too strongly in natural inequality. At the same time, he recognized the problem for what is was. His conclusion is particularly relevant to America in the mid twentieth century:

... nature has made a stamp on the American slave that is likely to prevent . . . consummation, and which menaces much future ill to the country. The time must come when American slavery shall cease, and when that day shall arrive, (unless early and effectual means are devised to obviate it,) two races will exist in the same region, whose feelings will be embittered by inextinguishable hatred, and who carry on their faces, the respective stamps of their factions. The struggle that will follow, will necessarily be a war of extermination. The evil day may be delayed, but can scarcely be averted.

Such near-prophetic remarks can be easily understood and appreciated today. Yet at other times Cooper's economy of style tends to obscure the full extent of his insight. As he notes in the introduction, his concern was more to present a wide range of subjects connected with American democracy than to write profoundly on each. He rarely covers topics comprehensively, but his individual sentences or passages often convey a great deal of meaning. Consider, for example, his comment upon the need to restrain majority rule:

Were the majority of a country to rule without restraint, it is probable as much injustice and oppression would follow, as are found under the dominion of one. It belongs to the nature of men to arrange themselves in parties, to lose sight of truth and justice in partizanship and prejudice, to mistake their own impulses for that which is proper, and to do wrong because they are indisposed to seek the right. Were it wise to trust power, unreservedly, to majorities, all fundamental and controlling laws would be unnecessary, since they might, as occasion required, emanate from the will of numbers. Constitutions would be useless.

Although the need for restraint was certainly not a new idea when Cooper wrote, he comes very close in a few words to the heart of modern discussions of constitutionalism. On other points, Cooper is equally concise but informative.

In terms of contemporary society, however, *The American Democrat* contains observations of even greater significance. In the first place, Cooper puts a great deal of stress on the need to distinguish between myth and reality. At a time when the former is often mistaken for the latter, when mass communications media and advertising do their best to make the unreal seem real, and when the concept of 'doublethink' is no longer limited to fiction, Cooper's warning is especially pertinent. It is here that his suggestion of an alternative title to the book has particular meaning, for Cooper's primary concern was to dismiss and discredit cant. He wanted to describe things as they were rather than as they might be made to seem. He stressed the way in which governments can claim to one character whilst taking on quite another; he noted, for example, that the façade of monarchy in Britain in fact concealed government by aristocracy. The pretensions of government, he suggested, are frequently belied by the facts, and the principles of a particular society may have little to do with its practices.

It is particularly refreshing, in view of the self-congratulatory tone of so many works on American democracy, to have Cooper's penetrating and critical comments on the bases of democratic self-government. He wanted to show the way the term 'the people' might be misused to give a totally false impression, and his analysis of the nature of the written constitution ('On the Republick of the United

States of America') cuts quickly to the core. He states concisely how the constitution was adopted and makes it obvious that 'we the people' is more a matter of propaganda than of fact. His discussion of sovereignty is similarly realistic. If the word was to have any meaning at all (and that point itself might be arguable), it was ridiculous for the states to consider themselves sovereign after having given up so many powers. Individual states could be no match for a national government which had gained the power to make war and peace, control foreign relations, control commerce, and coin money, to name only a few examples. Although nations sometimes exist as much on myth as on reality, the acceptance of the common-sense nature of Cooper's descriptions might have saved the nation, perhaps not from a bloody civil war, but at least from a century of tortuous reasoning by the Supreme Court which through the concept of 'dual sovereignty' was able effectively to check all types of neeessary governmental action.

Cooper's attempt to distinguish between what is substance and what façade made it clear that democracy was not the panacea that many had claimed it to be. He was, as has been pointed out, a convinced democrat. He believed in democracy because 'Though majorities often decide wrong, it is believed that they are less liable to do so than minorities.' At the same time, he recognized innumerable difficulties, and he was not one to suggest that the people could do no wrong, or that the cure for the ills of democracy was more democracy. Rather, he suggested the need in democracies for means to be devised to keep the majority within recognized and determined bounds. The people, he pointed out, are their own worst enemies in a democracy, and they must be restrained from harming themselves; hence his argument that constitutionalism is as vital to decent government as is majority rule. Hence also his concern for established procedures and institutions:

51

It ought to be impressed on every man's mind, in letters of brass, '*That, in a democracy, the publick has no power that is not expressly conceded by the institutions, and that this power, moreover, is only to be used under the forms prescribed by the constitution. All beyond this, is oppression, when it takes the character of acts, and not unfrequently when it is confined to opinion.*' [Cooper's italics.]

The relevance of Cooper's efforts to distinguish between façade and substance, words and things, is beyond question. To much of the world America has become the very symbol of resistance to change, but internally emphasis is placed on the responsiveness and adaptability of institutions. Policy decisions which might be perfectly acceptable on the basis of national self-interest must often be rationalized on the basis of universal norms of behaviour. And while the principles of national self-determination are acclaimed in the abstract, the United States on more than one occasion has refused to allow particular nations to apply them. The growth in the second half of this century of political alienation may very well be a product of disillusionment resulting from growing evidence of the gap between professed principles and realpolitik.

What may be even more worrying is the increasing difficulty of discerning the difference between truth and reality. Consider how frequently American policy is discussed, both by governmental institutions and by the press, in terms of *images*. Presidential campaigns, questions of war and peace, and domestic policy as well are frequently discussed not on the basis of their merits, but on the image a particular action is likely to present to Americans or to the rest of the world. The word *image* itself denotes unreality; yet this has become one of the touchstones of modern decision-making.

Cooper would have found this trend discreditable and dangerous. He was committed to opposing hypocrisy and cant, but apparently they have now become essential features of the American political system. There is often less concern for presentation of fact than for creation of illusion. Even the skills of professional public relations firms have been brought in to help with that task. To Cooper, as was noted earlier, the American democrat without truth is nothing. The idea of truth is, of course, more elusive and less certain than when Cooper wrote, but the need remains to seek reality beneath the 'fulsome, false and meretricious eulogiums' which bury it. It is ironic that the twentieth century has seen the development of those mass communications media which would make possible total dissemination of accurate information but which are too often the very means of masking reality.

The American Democrat suggests two facets of the problem of information. The first concerns sources of information. In many ways that problem was not as great in Cooper's day as it is in our own. When the danger to democracy lay in the possibility of legislative domination, truth would have been harder to conceal, for secrecy is hardly the strongest asset of legislative assemblies. More recently, however, the executive has become the dominant figure in American government, and he is in a good position to disclose only what he likes, for secrets are always kept better by one person than by many. And the presidential advantage is increased by the force of circumstance. It was argued in *The Federalist* that the executive must be given control of foreign affairs, for that field more than any other demands the secrecy, unity, and dispatch which only executives can provide. Needless to say, as foreign relations and defence play an increasingly large part in national life, the power of the President is increased accordingly. Very frequently, the public have no choice but to accept the information granted them, while in instance after instance that has later been shown to be false.

The second aspect of information considered by Cooper is whether the public will accept the truth even when it is offered. He noted that Americans are peculiarly reluctant to accept truths about their own society and tend to be very thin-skinned about criticism. That argument has not lost its validity. Years of argument were not sufficient to make the country realize the importance of equal rights for Negroes. Descriptions of poverty in America have been countered by flat denials. Faith in a free society is sustained despite innumerable attempts, many successful, to impose restrictions on political expression. The principle of national self-determination is continually espoused in the face of actions which on the part of any other nation would have been instantly condemned by America as imperialist. These represent precisely the type of cant Cooper wished to expose.

The second major point on which *The American Democrat* holds particular meaning for the twentieth century is the need to distinguish democracy from egalitarianism. It should certainly be apparent from the foregoing that Cooper was a democrat by conviction if not by birth. He believed that a majority of the electorate, if properly constrained by constitutional limitations, was the safest repository for political power. Moreover, he believed that the electorate should comprise a large segment of the population, even if he did not advocate a suffrage as wide as that existing today. At the same time, Cooper was unwilling to concede that political equality required conformity to the norms of mediocrity. He supported the idea that men should help to determine the way in which they are governed, but he recognized amongst men natural differences which he had no desire to see reduced to uniformity.

In a nation so obsessed with notions of equality, it took an act of courage to point out its limitations. However closely connected democracy and *political* equality may be, Cooper was concerned to show the dangers of insisting upon an indiscriminate equality in every sphere. He was disturbed in the first place by its levelling impact. Although inequality of wealth has long been justified by the myth of equal opportunity, there is a reluctance in American society to recognize any other kind of dissimilarity. Once it is assumed that one man is as good as another for purposes of voting, it is easy to be misled into believing that the maxim applies to other fields as well. It was to that extension that Cooper took exception, and he tried to indicate the inevitability of certain kinds of inequality.

He also wanted to show that the levelling effect of fierce egalitarianism might well lead to restriction of personal freedom. Complete equality demands conformity to majority norms, and any divergence is suspect. When no man can differ substantially from his neighbours, the result is a deadening conformity, and an aroused majority opinion is sufficiently powerful to punish any deviation, whatever the legal guarantees. 'Witch-hunts' have been the inevitable by-products throughout much of American history. Like Hamilton before him, Cooper had reason to fear the intolerance of the masses encouraged by the concept of equality to believe their ideas to be the correct ones.

Cooper believed in a democratic society, but he hoped it would be possible to achieve within it a dignified and urbane culture as well. His criticisms were directed to the achievement of that combination, and it remains a highly desirable goal.

SUGGESTIONS FOR FURTHER READING

Chief Political Works by Cooper

STUDIES AND COMMENTARIES

1. *Notions of the Americans* (1828)
2. *Letter to General Lafayette* (1831)
3. *A Letter to His Countrymen* (1834)
4. *Gleanings in Europe:*
   Switzerland (1836)
   The Rhine (1836)
   England (1837)
   Italy (1838)
5. *The American Democrat* (1838)
6. *The Chronicles of Cooperstown* (1838)
7. *New York* (unfinished at the time of Cooper's death and first published, in part, in the New York magazine *Spirit of the Fair*; other fragments first published by J. F. Beard, Jr, in *New York Historical Society Quarterly* (April 1953), Vol. XXXVII, No. 2, pp. 109–45)
8. *Letters and Journals of James Fenimore Cooper*, ed. J. F. Beard, Jr (Cambridge, Mass., 1960–68), 6 vols.

POLITICAL FICTION

1. *Lionel Lincoln* (1825)
2. *The Bravo* (1831)
3. *The Heidenmauer* (1832)
4. *The Headsman* (1833)
5. *The Monikins* (1835)
6. *Home as Found* (1838)
7. *Autobiography of a Pocket Handkerchief* (1843)
8. *Satanstoe* (1845)
9. *The Chainbearer* (1845)
10. *The Redskins* (1846)
11. *The Crater* (1847)

12. *The Ways of the Hour* (1850)
13. *The Lake Gun* (1850)

Works About Cooper

RELEVANT GENERAL WORKS

1. Grossman, James, *James Fenimore Cooper* (New York, 1949)
2. Spiller, R. E., *Fenimore Cooper: Critic of His Times* (New York, 1931)
3. Spiller, R. E., 'Second Thoughts on Cooper as Social Critic' in *James Fenimore Cooper: A Re-Appraisal,* ed. Mary Cunningham (Cooperstown, 1954), pp. 172–89
4. Spiller, R. E., and Philip Blackburn, *A Descriptive Bibliography of the Writings of James Fenimore Cooper* (New York, 1934)

STUDIES OF COOPER'S POLITICAL VIEWS

1. Beard, J. F., Jr, Introduction to *Letters and Journals of James Fenimore Cooper* (Cambridge, Mass., 1960), Vol. I, pp. xvii–xxxiv
2. Becker, George, 'James Fenimore Cooper and American Democracy', *College English* (March 1956), Vol. XVII, No. 6, pp. 325–34
3. Bewley, Marius, *The Eccentric Design* (London, 1959), pp. 47–112
4. Dekker, George, *James Fenimore Cooper the Novelist* (London, 1967), pp. 1–19, 104–12, 127–60, 218–59
5. Kirk, Russell, *The Conservative Mind* (London, 1954), pp. 176–82
6. Mencken, H. L., Introduction to *The American Democrat* (New York, 1931, 1956)
7. Meyers, Marvin, *The Jacksonian Persuasion* (Stanford, 1957), pp. 42–75
8. Outland, Ethel, *The 'Effingham' Libels on Cooper* (Madison, 1929)
9. Parrington, V. L., *Main Currents in American Thought* (New York, 1927), Vol. II, pp. 222–37
10. Philbrick, Thomas, Introduction to *The Crater* (Cambridge, Mass., 1962)

SUGGESTIONS FOR FURTHER READING

11. Schlesinger, Arthur M., Jr, *The Age of Jackson* (London, 1946), pp. 375–80
12. Spiller, R. E., Introductory Note to *The American Democrat* (New York, 1956)
13. Waples, Dorothy, *The Whig Myth of James Fenimore Cooper* (New Haven, 1938)

CHRONOLOGY OF
JAMES FENIMORE COOPER

1754   William Cooper born in Pennsylvania.

1786   William Cooper founds Cooperstown on the edge of Lake Otsego in New York.

1789   James Cooper born (15 September) at Burlington, New Jersey. [Inauguration of George Washington as first President.]

1790   William Cooper's family moves to Cooperstown.

1796–1800   [Period of Federalist supremacy: John Adams as U.S. President, John Jay as Governor of New York, William Cooper as U.S. Congressman.]

1803   James Cooper enters Yale College.

1805   Expelled from Yale because of misconduct.

1806–7   Sails before the mast on the *Stirling* to England and Spain.

1808   Becomes midshipman in U.S. Navy; service at Fort Oswego (Lake Ontario) and New York City; retires from active service shortly after.

1809   Death of William Cooper.

1811   Marriage to Susan Augusta De Lancey.

1811–19   Gentleman farmer in Cooperstown and Westchester Co., New York.

1820-22   Begins participating actively in politics and literature, as Secretary to Westchester Co. Clintonian Republicans and as author of *Precaution* (1820) and *The Spy* (1821).

1822–6   Moves to New York City and sets up as professional writer: *The Pioneers* (1823), *The Pilot* (1824), *Lionel Lincoln* (1825), *The Last of the Mohicans* (1826). [John Adams elected President, 1824.]

1826–33   Residence in Europe: based mainly in Paris but with extended visits in England, Switzerland, Germany, the Low Countries, and especially Italy. The period of Cooper's involvement in English, French, and Polish politics through his friendships with such figures as Lord William Russell, Lafayette, and Adam Mickiewicz. [Andrew Jackson elected President, 1828 and 1832.] Publishes *The Prairie* (1827), *The Red Rover* (1827), *Notions of the Americans* (1828), *The Wept of Wish-ton-Wish* (1829), *The Water Witch* (1830), *The Bravo* (1831), *The Heidenmauer* (1832), *and The Headsman* (1833).

1833–6   Residence in New York City: period during which Cooper's disillusionment with the American reading public and distrust of the 'oligarchical' (Whig) party, already pronounced before he left Europe, leads him to stop writing novels. Becomes an active supporter of the Jacksonian party. *A Letter to His Countrymen* (1834), *The Monikins* (1835).

1836   Returns to the home of his father, Otsego Hall, in Cooperstown. Commences publication of five volumes of European travels (1836–8). [Van Buren succeeds Jackson as President.]

1837–8   Three Mile Point affair leads to publication of *Homeward Bound* and *Home as Found* (1838) and libel suits against Whig editors. [W. H. Seward elected N.Y. Governor, 1838.] *American Democrat* (1838) and *Chronicles of Cooperstown* (1838).

1839   *History of the Navy of the United States*. [Outbreak of Anti-Rent troubles on the Rensselaer estates near Albany.]

1840–43   Begins writing historical romances again: *The Pathfinder* (1840), *Mercedes of Castile* (1840), *The Deerslayer* (1841), *The Two Admirals* (1842), *Wing-and-Wing* (1842), *Wyandotte* (1843). [Election of Harrison as President and re-election of Seward in 1840; Tyler becomes President in 1841.]

1844–7   Supports landlords in the Anti-Rent controversy and President Polk [elected in 1844] in the war with Mexico. *Afloat and Ashore* and *Miles Wallingford* (1844). The 'Littlepage Trilogy': *Satanstoe* (1845), *The Chainbearer* (1845), and *The Redskins* (1846). *Jack Tier* (1846–8). *The Crater* (1847).

1848–50   Supports Compromise measures of 1850 and publishes last novels: *The Oak Openings* (1849), *The Sea Lions* (1849), and *The Ways of the Hour* (1850). [Taylor elected President in 1848, succeeded by Fillmore in 1850; Seward elected U.S. Senator.]

1851   Cooper dies (14 September) in Cooperstown, leaving his last work, *The Towns of Manhattan*, unfinished.

NOTE ON THE TEXT

This edition reproduces without correction or alteration the text of the first edition, which was published by H. and E. Phinney in Cooperstown, New York, in 1838. This was the only edition published during Cooper's lifetime.

THE

AMERICAN DEMOCRAT,

OR

HINTS ON THE SOCIAL AND CIVIC RELATIONS
OF THE UNITED STATES OF AMERICA.

————————

BY

J. FENIMORE COOPER.

————————

COOPERSTOWN:
H. & E. PHINNEY.
1838.

Introduction

THIS little work has been written, in consequence of its author's having had many occasions to observe the manner in which principles that are of the last importance to the happiness of the community, are getting to be confounded in the popular mind. Notions that are impracticable, and which if persevered in, cannot fail to produce disorganization, if not revolution, are widely prevalent, and while many seem disposed to complain, few show a disposition to correct them. In those instances in which efforts are made to persist or to advance the innovations of the times, the writers take the extremes of the disputed points, the one side looking as far behind it, over ground that can never be retrod, as the other looks ahead, in the idle hope of substituting a fancied perfection for the ills of life. It is the intention of this book to make a commencement towards a more just discrimination between truth and prejudice. With what success the task has been accomplished, the honest reader will judge for himself.

The Americans are obnoxious to the charge of tolerating gross personalities, a state of things that encourages bodies of men in their errors while it oppresses individuals, and which never produced good of any sort, at the very time they are nationally irritable on the subject of common failings. This is reversing the case as it exists in most civilized countries, where personalities excite disgust, and society is deemed fair game. This weakness in the American character might easily be accounted for, but, the object being rather to amend than to explain, the body of the work is referred to for examples.

Power always has most to apprehend from its own illusions. Monarchs have incurred more hazards from the follies of their own that have grown up under the adulation of parasites, than from the machinations of their enemies; and, in a democracy, the delusion that would elsewhere be poured into the ears of the prince, is poured into those of the people. It is hoped that this work, while free from the spirit of partizanship, will be thought to be exempt from this imputation.

The writer believes himself to be as good a democrat as there is in America. But his democracy is not of the impracticable school. He prefers a democracy to any other system, on account of its comparative advantages, and not on account of its perfection. He knows it has evils; great and increasing evils, and evils peculiar to itself; but he believes that monarchy and aristocracy have more. It will be very apparent to all who read this book, that he is not a believer in the scheme of raising men very far above their natural propensities.

A long absence from home, has, in a certain degree, put the writer in the situation of a foreigner in his own country; a situation probably much better for noting peculiarities, than that of one who never left it. Two things have struck him painfully on his return; a disposition in the majority to carry out the opinions of the system to extremes, and a disposition in the minority to abandon all to the current of the day, with the hope that this current will lead, in the end, to radical changes. Fifteen years since, all complaints against the institutions were virtually silenced, whereas now it is rare to hear them praised, except by the mass, or by those who wish to profit by the favors of the mass.

In the midst of these conflicting opinions, the voice of simple, honest, and what, in a country like this, ought to be fearless, truth, is nearly smothered; the one party effecting its ends by fulsome, false and meretricious eulogiums, in which it does not itself believe, and the other giving utterance to its discontent in useless and unmanly complaints.

It has been the aim of the writer to avoid both these errors also.

No attempt has been made to write very profound treatises on any of the subjects of this little book. The limits and object of the work forbade it; the intention being rather to present to the reader those opinions that are suited to the actual condition of the country, than to dwell on principles more general. A work of the size of this might be written on the subject of 'Instruction' alone, but it has been the intention to present reasons and facts to the reader, that are peculiarly American, rather than to exhaust the subjects.

Had a suitable compound offered, the title of this book would have been something like 'Anti-Cant,' for such a term expresses the intention of the writer, better, perhaps, than the one he has actually chosen. The work is written more in the spirit of censure than of praise, for its aim is correction; and virtues bring their own reward, while errors are dangerous.

Contents

CONTENTS

On Government

MAN is known to exist in no part of the world, without certain rules for the regulation of his intercourse with those around him. It is a first necessity of his weakness, that laws, founded on the immutable principles of natural justice, should be framed, in order to protect the feeble against the violence of the strong; the honest from the schemes of the dishonest; the temperate and industrious, from the waste and indolence of the dissolute and idle. These laws, though varying with circumstances, possess a common character, being formed on that consciousness of right, which God has bestowed in order that men may judge between good and evil.

Governments have many names, which names, in all cases, are dependent on some one of the leading features of the institutions. It is usual, however, to divide governments into despotisms, limited monarchies, and republicks; but these terms are too vague to answer the objects of definitions, since many aristocracies have existed under the designation of monarchies, and many monarchies have been styled republicks.

A despotism is a government of absolute power, in which the entire authority is the possession of the prince. The term 'despot,' as applied to a sovereign, however, is not properly one of reproach. It merely signifies a ruler who is irresponsible for his acts, and who governs without any legal restraint on his will. The word 'tyrant' had originally the same meaning, though, in a measure, both have become so far corrupted as to convey an idea of abuses.

A limited monarchy is a government in which the will of the sovereign is restrained by certain provisions of the

state, that cannot lawfully be violated. In its true signification, the word monarch means any prince at the head of a
state. Monarchs are known by different titles; such as em-
perors, kings, princes, grand dukes, dukes, &c. &c.; but it is
not now common to apply the term to any below the rank of
kings. The title of sovereign is of more general use, though
properly meaning the same thing as that of monarch.

A republick is a government in which the pervading
acknowledged principle is the right of the community as
opposed to the right of a sovereign. In other words, the
term implies the sovereignty of the people, in lieu of that
of a monarch. Thus nations which have possessed kings,
dukes, and princes at their heads, have been termed republicks, because they have reserved the right to elect the
monarchs; as was formerly the case in Poland, Venice,
Genoa, and in many other of the Italian states, in particular.
Even Napoleon continued to style France a republick, after
he had assumed the imperial diadem, because his elevation
to the throne was sanctioned by the votes of the French
nation. The term, in his case, however, was evidently misapplied, for the crown was made hereditary in his family,
while the polity of a republick supposes a new election on
the death of the last ruler, if not oftener. In the case of
Napoleon, the people elected a dynasty, rather than a
prince.

In a republick the chief of the state is always elective.
Perhaps this fact is the most accurate technical distinction
between a monarchy and this form of government, though
the pervading principle of the first is the right of the sovereign, and of the last the right of the community. The term
republick, (*respublica) means the public things, or the
common weal. Hence the term commonwealth, the word
wealth, in its political sense, meaning prosperity in general,
and not riches in particular.

If these theoretical distinctions were rigidly respected, it

* *Res*, a thing; *publica*, public – 'public things.'

would be easy to infer the real character of a government from its name; but nothing can be less alike than governments ordinarily are, in their action, and in their professions. Thus despotism can scarcely be said to exist in truth, in any part of christendom; monarchs being compelled to govern according to established laws, which laws are formed on principles reasonably just, while they are restrained in the exercise of their will by an opinion that has been created by the advanced intelligence of the age.

Some kings are monarchs only in name, the power having essentially passed into the hands of a few of their nominal subjects; and, on the other hand, some princes, who, by the constitutional principles of the system, are deemed to be but a part of the state, effectually control it, by means of bribes, rewards, and political combinations, submitting to little more restraint than the nominal despots. Just at this time, Prussia is an instance of the first of these truths, England of the second, and France of the last.

Prussia, though a despotism in theory, is governed as mildly, and, apart from political justice, as equitably and legally, as any other country. The will of the sovereign is never made to interfere, arbitrarily, with the administration of law, and the law itself proceeds from the principles that properly influence all legislation, though it can only receive its authority from the will of the king. That country furnishes a proof of the progress of opinion, as well as of its power to check abuses. It was only the great grandfather of the present sovereign who caused tall men to marry tall women at his command, in order to gratify a silly desire to possess a regiment of the tallest troops in the world. The influence of opinion on governments has been greatly aided by the wars and revolutions of the last, and of the present century, in which privileges have been diminished, and the rights, as well as, what is perhaps of more importance, the knowledge of their rights among the people, have been greatly augmented.

England, which is called a monarchy, is in fact a complicated but efficient aristocracy. Scarcely one of the powers that is attributed to the king by the constitution, and which were in truth exercised by his predecessors, is possessed by the present monarch in fact. By the constitution, the king of England is supposed to form a balance between the nobles and the people, whereas, in truth, his utmost influence is limited to holding a balance between parties, and this only in cases of a nearly equal force between contending factions. The extent of the authority of the king of England, at the present day, amounts to little more than the influence which he is permitted to use in minor cases, the aristocracy having devised expedients to control him on all occasions that are deemed of moment. As the mode in which this change has been effected, illustrates the manner in which governments are made to take one character, while they profess to belong to another, a brief exposition will aid the reader in understanding the subject.

The king of England can do no wrong, but the ministers are responsible to parliament. As the country has no written constitution, and laws enacted by the king, lords and commons, have the force of constitutional provisions, a system has been established, by taking advantage of the necessities of different sovereigns, by which no executive act is legal, that is not sanctioned by at least one responsible minister. It follows, the monarch can do nothing to which his parliament is seriously opposed, since no minister will incur the risk of its displeasure. It is true that the nominal assent of the king is necessary to the enactment of a law, but the ministers being responsible for the consequences if it is withheld, and the parliament alone being the judge of these consequences, as well as of the criminals, while it has an active jealousy of its own power, no instance of the exercise of this authority has occurred for more than a century. The right to withold supplies has been the most efficient agent of the parliament, in subduing the authority of the crown.

By the theory of the British constitution, the king can declare war. Formerly this prerogative was exercised by different warlike sovereigns for personal motives. Now, the right exists only in name, for no minister would consent to give the declaration the legal forms, with the certainty of being impeached, and punished, unless acting in accordance with the wishes of parliament.

Although parliament exercises this authority in all cases of importance, the ministers are permitted to perform most minor acts of authority unquestioned, so long as they have a party in the legislature to sustain them. This party, however, is necessary to their remaining in the ministry, and it follows that the majority of parliament controls the very appointment of ministers, the only important political function that the king can now, even in theory, exercise without the intervention of a responsible minister. Were he, however, to appoint a minister in opposition to the wishes of parliament, that body would refuse the required laws. The first requisite, therefore, on the formation of a new ministry, is to enquire who can 'meet parliament', as it is termed; or, in other words, what ministers will be agreeable to a majority of the legislature.

Thus, while the king of England says who shall be his ministers, the parliament says who they shall not be; and, in this instance, supported as it is by a control of all legislation, the negative power is found to be stronger than the affirmative. In reality, the ministers of Great-Britain are appointed by the parliament of the country, and not by the king, and this is virtually neutralizing, if not directly annihilating, all the available authority of the latter.

In theory, the government of France and that of Great-Britain have the same general character. In practice, however, owing to the greater political advancement of the last of these two countries, France, to-day, is not far from the point where England stood a century since. Then the king of England ruled through his parliament, whereas now the parliament rules through the king. On the other hand, with much of the machinery of a free state, the king of the French governs himself. A dread of the people's getting the ascendancy, causes the aristocracy to lend itself to the power of the crown, which not only dictates the law, but, in many cases, proves to be stronger than the law itself. Of the three countries, perhaps legality is more respected in Prussia and Austria, both despotisms in theory, than in France, which has the profession of a limited monarchy. This difference is owing to the security of the two first governments, and to the insecurity of the last.

These facts show the necessity of distinguishing between names and things in governments, as well as in other matters. The institutions of no country are rigidly respected in practice, owing to the cupidity and passions of men; and vigilance in the protection of principles is even more necessary in a democracy than in a monarchy, as their violation is more certain to affect the interests of the people under such a form of government than under any other. A violation of the principles of a democracy is at the loss of the people, while, in a monarchy, it is usually their gain.

On Republicks

REPUBLICS have been as liable to frauds, and to departures from their professions, as any other polities, though no government can properly be termed a republick at all, in which the predominant authority of a single hereditary ruler is acknowledged. In all republicks there must be more or less of direct representation, however much its influence is lessened by the duration and by the magnitude of the trusts.

Poland was formerly termed a republick, because the kingly office was elective, and on account of the power of the

Diet. At that time any member of this body could defeat a law by exclaiming in Latin, *Veto*, (I forbid it,) from which usage the word *veto* has been adopted as a substantive, in most of the languages of christendom, to express the same power in the different executive rulers; which it is now common to term the 'veto-power.' The exercise of this right was found so inconvenient in practice, that, at length, in cases of gravity, the nobles of the Diet would draw their swords, and menace the dissenting member with death, unless he withdrew his 'veto'. As a negative authority often has the efficiency of that which is affirmative, it is scarcely possible to conceive of a system in which the will of a majority was less consulted than in this.

The republick of Venice was an hereditary aristocracy, as, in a great measure, was that of ancient Rome. The term, in its true signification, perhaps, infers a free government, for it means a representation of the general interests of the state, but, as in practice, this representation became confined purely to the interests of the state, and the state itself was under the control of a few who did not fail to turn their authority to their private advantage, the system has oftener resulted in abuses than even that of monarchies. The profession of a free government, in which the facts do not frankly concur, usually tends to gross wrongs, in order to conceal and protect the frauds. In Venice, such was the jealousy and tyranny of the state, that a secret council existed, with an authority that was almost despotick, while it was inquisitorial, and which was removed from the usual responsibility of opinion, by an expedient that was devised to protect its members from the ordinary liabilities of common censure. This council consisted of three nobles, who held their office for a limited period, and were appointed by drawing lots, each person concealing the fact of the lot's having fallen on himself, until he met his associates at an appointed place It is an extraordinary fact, that the same expedient was devised to conceal the murderers, in the well known case of Morgan, who fell a victim to the exaggeration and weakness of some of the members of the Masonic Fraternity.

By examining the different republicks of ancient and modern times, it would be found that most of them had little more than the profession of liberty, though all substituted in them the right of the community for that of a monarch, as a primary principle. This feature, then, must be taken as the distinction between this form of government and that of kingdoms, or of the sovereignties in which one rules, or is supposed to rule.

Republicks may be aristocratical, or democratical; and they may so nearly approach both, as to render it matter of doubt to which class they properly belong; for the political combinations of communities, in a practical sense, are so numerous as almost to defeat accurate general definitions.

On the Republick of
the United States of America

THE government of the United States, differs from all others that have preceded it, though some imitations have been attempted in the southern parts of this continent. Its novelty, no less than its complicated nature, arising from its double system, has given birth to many errors in relation to its principles and its action, even among its own citizens, as well as among strangers.

The policy of the United States is that of a confederated republick, but the power of the federal government acting in most instances on the body of the community, without the intervention of the several states, it has been better styled a Union. This word, which is original as applied to a political system, was first given to this form of confederation, and is intended to express the greater intimacy of the relations of the parties, than those of all previous examples. It exists in the constitution, however, only as it is used in setting forth the motives for substituting that instrument for the old articles of confederation: the constitution being silent as to the particular polity of the country, except as it recognizes the general term of a republick.

The word constitution, of itself, properly implies a more identified form of government, than that which is usually understood to exist under confederation; the first inferring a social compact, fundamental and predominant, the last a league between independent sovereignties. These distinctions have a certain weight, though they are rather arbitrary than logical, since men may create any degree of allegiance, or of liability they may deem expedient, under any form, or modes of government. To deny this is to deny to bodies of human beings the right of self-government, a gift of nature. Though possessing a common end, governments are, in reality, subject to no laws but those of their own establishing.

The government of the United States was formed by the several states of the Union, as they existed at the period when the constitution was adopted, and one of its leading principles is, that all power which is not granted to the federal authority, remain in the states themselves, or what is virtually the same thing, in the people of the states. This principle follows as a necessary consequence from the nature of the grants to the federal government, but it has been clearly expressed in a clause of the instrument, that was introduced by way of amendment, in 1801. This feature distinguishes this federal government from all the federal governments that have gone before it, as it was the general and ancient rule that liberty existed as a concession from authority; whereas, here, we find authority existing as a concession from the ruled. Something like the same principle exists in the governments of the several states, and it once existed in the ancient democracies, though, in no other known system perhaps, as clearly and as unequivocally as in this, since it is a general maxim that governments should have all power, however much they may restrain themselves in its exercise.

In the conflict of parties, the question by whom the federal government was formed, has been agitated with more seriousness than the point at issue merited, since, the fact admitted that the power which framed it did not exceed its authority, it is much more essential to know what was done, than to ascertain who did it. The notion that the *people* of the United States, in the popular signification of the word, framed the government, is contrary to fact, and leads to a wrong interpretation of many of the distinctive features of the system. The constitution of the United States was formed by a convention composed of delegates elected by the different states, in modes prescribed by their several laws and usages. These delegates voted by states, and not as individuals, and the instrument was referred back to conventions in the respective states for approval, or ratification. It is a governing principle of political maxims, that the power to ratify, is the power that possesses the authority in the last resort. Thus, treaties between independent sovereignties, are never valid until ratified by the high treaty-making powers of the respective countries. As the several states of this Union first acted through delegates of their own appointing, and then ratified their acts, in conventions also chosen by constituencies of their own selection, it is not easy to establish any thing more plainly than the fact, that the constitution of the United States was framed by the states then in existence, as communities, and not by the body of the people of the Union, or by the body of the people of the states, as has been sometimes contended.

In favor of the latter opinion, it is maintained that the several states were an identified nation previously to the formation of the government, and the preamble of the constitution itself, has been quoted to prove that the compact was formed by the *people*, as distinct from the states. This preamble commences by saying that 'We the people of the United States,' for reasons that are then set forth, have framed the instrument that follows; but in respecting a form of phraseology, it, of necessity, neither establishes a fact, nor sets up a principle, and when we come to examine the collateral circumstances, we are irresistably led to regard it merely as a naked and vague profession.

That the several states were virtually parts of one entire nation previously to the formation of any separate general government, proves nothing in the premises, as the very circumstance that a polity distinct from that of Great Britain was established by our ancestors, who were members of the great community that was then united in one entire nation, sufficiently shows that these parts can separate, and act independently of each other. Such a circumstance might be, and probably it was, a strong motive for forming a more identified government, but it cannot properly be quoted as authority for, or against any of its provissions. The latter are a mere question of fact, and as such their construction must depend on their intention as explained in language.

The term 'people,' like most other substantives, has its general and its specific significations. In its general signification, the people of a country, means the population of a country; as the population of a country includes the women and children, nothing can be clearer than that the 'people,' in this signification, did not form the American constitution. The specific significations of this word are numerous, as rich, poor, wise, silly, good and bad people. In a political sense, the people means those who are vested with political rights, and, in this particular instance, the people vested with political rights, were the constituencies of the several states, under their various laws, modifications and constitutions, which is but another name for the governments of the states themselves. 'We the *people*,' as used in the preamble of the constitution, means merely, 'We the *constituen-cies* of the several states.'

It follows, that the constitution of the United States was formed by the states, and not by the people of the entire country, as contended; the term used in the preamble being used in contra-distinction to the old divine right of sovereigns, and as a mode of expressing the general republican character of the government. The states, by a prescribed majority, can also amend the constitution, altering any of its provisions, with the exception of that which guaranties the equal representation of the states in the senate. It might be shown, that states possessing a minority of all the people of the Union can alter the constitution, a fact, in itself, which proves that the government of the United States, though a republick, is not necessarily a popular government, in the broadest meaning of the word. The constitution leaves the real character of the institutions of the country, with the exception that it prohibits monarchies, to be settled by the several states themselves.

On the other hand, too much importance is attached to what is called the reserved sovereignties of the several states. A community can hardly be termed sovereign at all, which has parted with all the great powers of sovereignty, such as the control of foreign relations, the authority to make war and peace, to regulate commerce, to coin money, keep fleets and armies, with all the other powers that have been ceded by the states to the federal government. But, admitting that the rights reserved are sovereign in their ordinary nature, they are scarcely so in the conditions under which they are enjoyed, since, by an amendment of the constitution, a state may be deprived of most of them, without its own consent. A community so situated can scarcely be deemed sovereign, or even independent.

The habit of drawing particular inferences from general theories, in matters as purely practical as those of government, is at all times dangerous, and the safest mode of construing the constitution of the United States, is by looking only at the instrument itself, without adverting to other systems, except as they may serve to give the proper signification of the terms of that instrument, as these terms were understood at the time it was framed.

Many popular errors exist on the subject of the influence of the federal constitution on the rights and liberties of the citizen. The rights and liberties of the citizen, in a great degree, depend on the political institutions of the several states, and not on those of the Union. Many of these errors have arisen from mistaking the meaning of the language of the constitution. Thus, when the constitution says that no laws shall be passed abridging the rights of the citizen in any particular thing, it refers to the power which, under that particular constitution, has the authority to pass a law at all. This power, under the government of the United States, is Congress, and no other.

An example will better show the distinction. In art. 6th of the amendments to the constitution, we find the following clause: 'In all criminal prosecutions, the accused shall enjoy the right of a speedy and *public* trial, by an impartial *jury*,' &c. &c. &c. It is not the meaning of this provision of the constitution, that, under the laws of the several states, the citizen shall be entitled to a *public* trial by a *jury*, but that these privileges shall be assured to those who are accused of crimes against the laws of the United States. It is true, that similar privileges, as they are deemed essential to the liberties of their citizens, are assured to them by the constitutions of the several states, but this has been done by voluntary acts of their own, every state having full power, so far as the constitution of the United States has any control over it, to cause its accused to be tried in secret, or without the intervention of juries, as the people of that particular state may see fit.

There is nothing in the constitution of the United States, to prevent all the states, or any particular state, from possessing an established religion, from putting the press under the control of censors, from laying restrictions and penalties on the rights of speech, or from imposing most of the political and civil restraints on the citizen, that are imposed under any other form of government.

The guarantees for the liberties of the citizen, given by the constitution of the United States, are very limited, except as against the action of the government of the Union alone. Congress may not pass any law establishing a religion, or abridging the freedom of speech, or of the press, but the provisions of the constitution relating to these subjects, have no reference to the rights of the states. This distinction is very essential to a correct understanding of the institutions of the country, as many are misled on the subject. Some of the states, for example, are rigid in enforcing respect for the sabbath, and a popular notion has prevailed that their laws are unconstitutional, since the federal compact guaranties liberty of conscience. This guarantee, like most of the others of the same nature, is only against the acts of Congress, and not against the acts of the states themselves. A state may pass any law it please to restrain the abuses of the sabbath, provided it do not infringe on the provisions of its own constitution or invade a right conceded to the United States. It cannot stop the mail for instance, or the passage of troops in the service of the federal government, but it may stop all who are not thus constitutionally protected by the superior power of the Union.

This reading of the constitution is in conformity with all the rules of construction, but that it is right, can be shown from the language of the instrument itself. In article 1st, section 9th, clause 3d, we find this provision – 'No bill of attainder, or *ex post facto* law, shall be passed.' In article 1st, section 10th, clause 1st, which section is composed entirely of restraints on the power of the states, we find this provision – 'No *state* shall pass any bill of attainder, *ex post facto* law, &c. &c.' Had the provision of clause 3d, sect. 9th, been intended to limit the powers of the states, clause 1st, sect. 10th, would clearly have been unnecessary. The latter provision therefore, is one of the few instances, in which the power of the states themselves, is positively restrained by the constitution of the United States.

Although the several states have conceded to the United States most of the higher attributes of sovereignty, they have reserved to themselves nearly all of the functions that render governments free, or otherwise. In declaring war, regulating commerce, keeping armies and navies, coining money, which are all high acts of sovereignty, despotisms and democracies are alike; all forms of governments equally controlling these interests, and usually in the same manner.

The characters of institutions depend on the repositories of power, in the last resort. In despotisms the monarch is this repository; in aristocracies, the few; in democracies, the many. By the constitution of the United States, its government is composed of different representations, which are chosen, more or less directly, by the constituencies of the several states. As there is no common rule for the construction of these constituencies, their narrowness, or width, must depend on the fundamental laws of the states, themselves. It follows that the federal government has no fixed character, so far as the nature of its constituency is concerned, but one that may constantly vary, and which has materially varied since the commencement of the government, though, as yet, its changes have always been in the direction of popular rights.

The only distinctive restriction imposed by the constitution of the United States on the character of the state governments, is that contained in article 4th, section 4th, clause 1st, which guaranties to each state a republican form of government. No monarchy, therefore, can exist in this country, as existed formerly, and now exists, in the confederation of Germany. But a republican form of government is not necessarily a free government. Aristocracies are oftener republicks than any thing else, and they have been among the most oppressive governments the world has ever known.

No state can grant any title of nobility; but titles of nobility are oftener the consequence than the cause of narrow governments. Neither Venice, Poland, Genoa, Berne, (a canton of Switzerland,) nor most of the other narrow aristocracies of Europe, had any titular nobles, though some of these countries were afflicted by governments of great oppression. Any state of this Union, by altering its own constitution, may place the power of its own government, and, by consequence, its representation in the government of the United States, in any dozen families, making it perpetual and hereditary. The only guarantee against such an act is to be found in the discretion of the people of the several states, none of whom would probably part with power for such a purpose, and the check which the other states might hold over any one of their body, by amending the constitution. As this instrument now exists, however, there can be no reasonable doubts of the power of any one, or of all the states, so to alter their polities.

By considering these facts, we learn the true nature of the government, which may be said to have both a theoretical character, and one in fact. In theory, this character is vague, and, with the immaterial exception of the exclusion of a monarchy and the maintenance of the representative form, one altogether dependent on the policy of the states, by which it may be made a representative aristocracy, a representative democracy, or a union of the two. The government, in fact, is a near approach to that of a representative democracy, though it is not without a slight infusion from a few mild aristocracies. So long as slavery exists in the country, or, it were better to say, so long as the African race exists, some portion of this aristocratic infusion will probably remain.

Stress is laid on the foregoing distinctions, because the government of the Union is a compact between separate communities, and popular misconceptions on the nature of the institutions, in a nation so much controlled by popular opinion, not only lead to injustice, but may lead to dissension. It is the duty of every citizen to acquire just notions of the terms of the bargain before he pretends to a right to enforce them.

On Distinctive American Principles

DISTINCTIVE American principles as properly refer to the institutions of the states as to those of the Union. A correct notion of the first cannot be formed without keeping the latter constantly in view.

The leading distinctive principle of this country, is connected with the fact that all political power is strictly a trust, granted by the constituent to the representative. These representatives possess different duties, and as the greatest check that is imposed on them, while in the exercise of their offices, exists in the manner in which the functions are balanced by each other, it is of the last importance that neither class trespass on the trusts that are not especially committed to its keeping.

The machinery of the state being the same in appearance, in this country and in that from which we are derived, inconsiderate commentators are apt to confound their principles. In England, the institutions have been the result of those circumstances to which time has accidentally given birth. The power of the king was derived from violence, the monarch, before the act of succession, in the reign of Queen Anne, claiming the throne in virtue of the conquest by William, in 1060. In America, the institutions are the result of deliberate consultation, mutual concessions, and design. In England, the people may have gained by diminishing the power of the king, who first obtained it by force; but, in America, to assail the rightful authority of the executive, is attacking a system framed by the constituencies of the states, who are virtually the people, for their own benefit. No assault can be made on any branch of this government, while in the exercise of its constitutional duties, without assaulting the right of the body of the nation, which is the foundation of the whole polity.

In countries, in which executive power is hereditary, and clothed with high prerogatives, it may be struggling for liberty to strive to diminish its influence; but, in this republick, in which the executive is elective, has no absolute authority in framing the laws, serves for a short period, is responsible, and has been created by the people, through the states, for their own purposes, it is assailing the rights of that people, to attempt in any manner to impede its legal and just action.

It is a general law in politics, that the power most to be distrusted, is that which, possessing the greatest force, is the least responsible. Under the constitutional monarchies of Europe, (as they exist in theory, at least,) the king, besides uniting in his single person all the authority of the executive, which includes a power to make war, create peers, and unconditionally to name to all employments, has an equal influence in enacting laws, his veto being absolute; but, in America, the executive, besides being elective, is stripped of most of these high sources of influence, and is obliged to keep constantly in view the justice and legality of his acts, both on account of his direct responsibilities, and on account of the force of public opinion.

In this country, there is far more to apprehend from congress, than from the executive, as is seen in the following reasons:—Congress is composed of many, while the executive is one, bodies of men notoriously acting with less personal responsibilities than individuals; congress has power to enact laws, which it becomes the duty of the executive to see enforced, and the really legislative authority of a country is always its greatest authority; from the decisions and constructions of the executive, the citizen can always appeal to the courts for protection, but no appeal can lie from the acts of congress, except on the ground of unconstitutionality; the executive has direct personal responsibilities under the laws of the land, for any abuses of his authority, but the member of congress, unless guilty of open corruption, is almost beyond personal liabilities.

It follows that the legislature of this country, by the intention of the constitution, wields the highest authority under the least responsibility, and that it is the power most to be distrusted. Still, all who possess trusts, are to be diligently watched, for there is no protection against abuses without responsibility, nor any real responsibility, without vigilance.

Political partisans, who are too apt to mistake the impulses of their own hostilities and friendships for truths, have laid down many false principles on the subject of the duties of the executive. When a law is passed, it goes to the executive for execution, through the executive agents, and, at need, to the courts for interpretation. It would seem that there is no discretion vested in the executive concerning the constitutionality of a law. If he distrust the constitutionality of any law, he can set forth his objections by resorting to the veto; but it is clearly the intention of the system that the whole legislative power, in the last resort, shall abide in congress, while it is necessary to the regular action of the government, that none of its agents, but those who are especially appointed for that purpose, shall pretend to interpret the constitution, in practice. The citizen is differently situated. If he conceive himself oppressed by an unconstitutional law, it is his inalienable privilege to raise the question before the courts, where a final interpretation can be had. By this interpretation the executive and all his agents are equally bound to abide. This obligation arises from the necessity of things, as well as from the nature of the institutions. There must be somewhere a power to decide on the constitutionality of laws, and this power is vested in the supreme court of the United States, on final appeal.

When called on to approve a law, even though its principle should have been already pronounced on by the courts, the executive is independent. He is now a legislator, and can disregard all other constructions of the constitution, but those dictated by his own sense of right. In this character, to the extent of his veto-power, he is superior to the courts, which have cognizance of no more than each case as it is presented for their consideration. The president may approve of a law that the court has decided to be unconstitutional in principle, or he may veto a law that the court has decided to be constitutional in principle. The legislator himself, is compelled to submit to the interpretation of the court, however different his own views of the law may have been in passing it, but as soon as he comes to act again as a legislator, he becomes invested with all his own high duties and rights. The court cannot make the constitution, in any case; it only interprets the law. One court may decide differently from another, and instances often occur in which the same judges see reason to change their own decisions, and it would be, to the last degree, inexpedient, to give the court an authority beyond the necessity of the circumstances.

Although the court can render a law null, its power does not extend beyond the law already passed. Congress may re-enact it, as often as it please, and the court will still exercise its reason in rejecting it. This is the balance of the constitution, which invites inquiry, the constituencies of the states holding a legal authority to render that constitutional which the courts have declared to be unconstitutional, or vice versa, by amendments to the instrument itself; the supremacy of the court being merely temporary, conditional, and growing out of expediency and necessity.

It has been said that it is a vital principle of this government, that each of its branches should confine itself to the particular duties assigned it by the constitution, and in no manner exceed them. Many grave abuses have already arisen from loosing sight of this truth, and there is danger that the whole system will be perverted from its intention, if not destroyed, unless they are seasonably corrected. Of these, the most prevalent, the one most injurious to the public service, that which has been introduced the most on foreign and the least on American principles, is the practice of using the time and influence of the legislatures, for the purpose of acting on the public mind, with a view to affect the elections. The usage has already gained so much footing, as seriously to impede the course of legislation.

This is one of the cases, in which it is necessary to discriminate between the distinctive principles of our own government, and those of the government of the country from which we are derived. In England, by the mode in which the power of the executive has been curtailed, it is necessary that the ministerial contests should be conducted in the legislative bodies, but, in this country, such a course cannot be imitated, without the legislators' assuming an authority that does not belong to them, and without dispossessing the people, in some measure, of their rights. He who will examine the constitution for the powers of congress, will find no authority to pass resolutions on, or to waste the time, which is the property of the public, in discussing the matters, on which, after all, congress has no power to decide. This is the test of legislative authority. Congress cannot properly even discuss a subject, that congress cannot legally control, unless it be to ascertain its own powers. In cases that do not admit of question, this is one of the grossest abuses of the institutions, and ought to be classed with the usurpations of other systems.

There is a feeling connected with this subject, that it behoves every upright citizen cautiously to watch. He may be opposed to the executive, for instance, as a party-man, and yet have an immediate representative in congress, of his own particular way of thinking; and it is a weakness of humanity, under such circumstances, for one to connect himself most directly with his own immediate candidate, and to look on his political opponent with distrust. The jealousy created by this feeling, induces unreflecting men to imagine that curbing their particular representatives, in matters of this nature, is curtailing their own rights and disposes them to defend what is inherently wrong, on personal motives.

Political systems ought to be, and usually are, framed on certain great and governing principles. These principles cannot be perverted, or lost sight of, without perverting, or rendering nugatory the system itself; and, under a popular government, in an age like this, far more is to be apprehended from indirect attacks on the institutions, than from those which are direct. It is usual to excuse these departures from the right on the plea of human propensities, but human institutions are framed expressly to curb such propensities, and no truth is more salutary than that which is contained in the homely saying, that 'law makers should not be law breakers.'

It is the duty of the citizen to judge of all political acts on the great principles of the government, and not according to his own political partialities, or prejudices. His own particular representative is no more a representative of the people, than the representative of any other man, and one branch of the government is no more representative than another. All are to keep within their respective spheres, and it may be laid down as a governing maxim of the institutions, *that the representative who exceeds his trusts, trespasses on the rights of the people.*

All comparisons between the powers of the British parliament and those of congress are more than useless, since they are bodies differently constituted, while one is absolute, and the other is merely a special trustee for limited and defined objects.

In estimating the powers of congress, there is a rule that may be safely confided in, and which has been already hinted at. The powers of congress are express and limited. That body therefore, can have no right *to pass resolutions* other than those which effect their own police, or, in a moral sense, even to make speeches, except on subjects on which *they have a right to pass laws*. The instant they exceed these limits, they exceed the bounds of their delegated authority. By applying this simple test to their proceedings, any citizen may, in ordinary cases, ascertain how far the representatives of the nation abuse their trusts.

Liberty is not a matter of words, but a positive and important condition of society. Its great safeguards, after placing its foundations on a popular base, is in the checks and balances imposed on the public servants, and all its real friends ought to know that the most insidious attacks, are made on it by those who are the largest trustees of authority, in their efforts to increase their power.

The government of the United States has three branches. The executive, the legislative and the judicial. These several branches are independent of each other, though the first is intended to act as a check on the second, no law or resolution being legal that is not first submitted to the president for his approval. This check, however, does not render the first an integral part of the legislature, as laws and resolutions may be passed without his approval, by votes of two thirds.

In most constitutional monarchies, the legislatures, being originally secondary powers, were intended as checks on the action of the crown, which was possessed of the greatest, and, by consequence, of the most dangerous authority; whereas, the case is reversed in America, the executive using his veto as a check on congress. Such is the intention of the constitution, though the tactics of party, and the bitterness of opposition, have endeavored to interpret the instrument differently, by appealing to the ancient prejudices derived from England.

On the Powers of the Executive

THE president 'sees the laws faithfully executed.' In order to render this power efficient, he appoints to office and removes all officers, but the judges, and those whom they are authorized by congress to appoint, who form an independent portion of the government. As this has been a disputed authority, it may be well to explain it more distinctly.

The president *nominates* to the senate and with its 'advice and consent,' *appoints* all the officers of the government, with the exception of those whose appointment congress has authority to vest, by law, in the heads of departments, or in the courts of justice. The functionaries appointed by the courts of law are not removable, either directly, or indirectly, by the president, that branch of the government being independent, and not *executing*, but merely *interpreting* the laws. Although the president cannot remove the officers who are appointed by the heads of departments, he can remove those heads of departments themselves, thereby securing a prompt and proper execution of their duties. In this manner all the executive agents are subject to the supervisory power of the president, as, there can be no just doubt, was the intention of the constitution.

The right of the president to remove from office has been disputed, but on insufficient grounds. Unless the constitution shall be so interpreted as to give him this power, all officers must hold their places until removed by death, or impeachment, as it is clear no other branch of the state, separately, or in connection with a second, possesses this authority. A brief examination of the instrument will demonstrate this truth, the reader bearing in mind that there is now question, only, of those officers who are appointed by the executive, and not of those who are appointed by the courts of law, or the heads of departments.

The language of the constitution is as follows:—'He (the president) shall have power, by and with the advice and consent of the senate, to make treaties, provided two thirds of the senators concur; and he shall *nominate,* and, by and with the advice and consent of the senate, *appoint* ambassadors,' &c. &c. and all the other officers of the government, with the exceptions already named. From this phraseology it has been contended that, as the senate has a voice in appointing, it ought to have a voice in removing from office, the constitution leaving the latter authority entirely to construction.

In addition to the paragraph just quoted, we find that 'he (the president) shall *commission* all officers of the United States.' All the direct provisions of the constitution on this subject, are contained in these two parts of sections.

The pretension in behalf of the senate's voice in removals, is made under an erroneous notion of its power in appointments. The senate in no manner *appoints* to office. This is proved by the language of the constitution, which reads, by taking away the parenthetical part of the sentence, '*he* (the president) shall appoint,' &c. &c. In no other way, can grammar be made of the sentence. The president, therefore, and not the senate appoints to office, and by construction, the president decides on the removal. The consent of the senate, in the cases of treaties and offices, is a bestowal of authority on the president, alone, by which consent he receives a complete power to act in the premises, as he shall judge expedient. Thus a treaty is not ratified, because the senate approves of it, nor a citizen appointed to office because the senate consents to his appointment; the authority granted in both cases being given to the president, and not to the instrument in the case of a treaty, or to the individual in the case of an appointment. The president may refuse to ratify a treaty, which is the consummation of such a compact, or to commission an officer, which is his authority to act, after having received the consent of the senate, in both cases. The power of the senate is merely a negative power in appointments and in treaties, its dissent defeating the intention of the president, but its assent in no manner obliging him to adhere to his first resolution. Or, it would be better still to say, the senate has power to complete the authority of the president.

In some countries a parent negatives the marriage of the child. This is a similar case in principle, for when the father consents, he does not marry, but permits his child to perform the affirmative act.

The powers of the president are three-fold, in the cases of appointments. He 'nominates,' he 'appoints' and he 'commissions.' To nominate is to propose, or name; to appoint, is to determine in the mind, or, in this case to settle on consultation; and to commission, is to empower. The last act, is the one by which the nominee receives his authority, and it would seem to be a just construction that the authority which appoints and empowers should have the right to withdraw its commission.

They who object to this reasoning, say that the power to 'commission' is merely a ministerial power. No part of the constitution can be thus limited in its signification. All the powers of the executive named in the instrument, are strictly executive powers, and are to be construed solely on the great principles that regulate all executive authority. This is in conformity with the letter and spirit of the constitution, which has instituted this high office, not as a ministerial, but as an executive office.

The distinction between an executive and ministerial function is great and manifest. The last is positive, and limited by the provisions of the law to be executed; the first has a wide discretion, and is always to be interpreted on as liberal and broad principles, as the nature of the case will allow; it being the intention that high political considerations should have their due weight on the acts of such an agent. But a quotation from the constitution, itself, will show our meaning. The section which contains the power of the president to commission, is in these words: 'He (the president,) shall, from time to time, give to congress information of the state of the Union, and recommend to their consideration such measures *as he shall judge necessary and expedient;* he may, on extraordinary occasions, convene both houses, or either of them, and, in case of disagreement between them, with respect to the time of adjournment, he may adjourn them to such time *as he may think proper*; he shall receive ambassadors and other public ministers; he shall take care that the laws be faithfully executed; and *he shall commission* (empower, in an executive sense) *all the officers of the United States.'*

Each and all of these high functions are executive, and are to be discharged on the great principles of executive power. Thus the president is not *obliged* to 'receive ambassadors and other public ministers,' as they shall present themselves, like a mere minister of state, when the act is contrary to the interests and character of the nation; but he is the depository of that discretionary authority, to receive, or to reject them, which by the usages of nations and in the necessity of things, must somewhere abide in all governments. Under the confederation this power resided in congress; under the constitution it is the president. Were this function merely a ministerial function, the president would have no power to decline receiving a foreign agent, and the country would be destitute of a necessary means to protect the interests and dignity of the state.

On the same principle, the right to commission (or empower) as an executive right, in the absence of any specific fundamental law to the contrary, infers the right to withdraw that commission; or in other words to remove from office.

All the different powers of the president confirm this construction. He is commanded 'to take care that the laws be faithfully executed,' a duty than can be discharged in no other manner, than by displacing unworthy agents, and entrusting the authority to worthier; he nominates, or originates the appointment; with the consent of the senate he settles the matter in his own mind, or appoints; and according to the true and technical signification of the word, he commissions, or empowers; unless it be intended that all offices shall be held during good behaviour, he removes.

That the constitution did not intend that officers should be irremovable, is to be inferred from the fact that duties are assigned the president, that can be discharged in no other manner than by displacing delinquents; from the general usages of governments; and from the fact that certain officers are named, in the way of exceptions, as those who are to hold their trusts during good behaviour.

An example will show the necessity of this power's existing in the president. A collector is commanded to perform certain acts, which he neglects to do, to the great injury of the country. The executive is ordered by the constitution to take care that this, as well as the other laws, be faithfully executed. He admonishes the delinquent, who pertinaciously adheres to his illegal course. In what manner is the president to enforce the law? Impeachment is not in his power, in the first place; and in the next place, it does not enforce the law, but punishes the offender. He may, in some cases, order the law officers of the government to prosecute for penalties, perhaps, but the law officers may also refuse to do their duties, and thus the whole intention of the institutions would be set at naught.

Errors have arisen, on these subjects, by misconceiving the meaning of the terms. 'Nominate,' 'appoint' and 'commission,' are to be construed in their broadest significations, in an instrument as dignified and comprehensive as a constitution, and with strict reference to the general character of the functions with which they are connected, functions that are purely executive and in no manner ministerial. This is the only statesmanlike view of the question, though the practice of permitting common-law lawyers to expound the great national compact, has had the effect to narrow and degrade the instrument, favoring the views of political factions, and not unfrequently disturbing the country without a commensurate object.

The practice of the government has always been in conformity with this reasoning, though, it is believed that no commentator has ever given a sufficiently broad signification to the power to commission. If this power be strictly executive, as it is just to deem it, it must be taken like the power to receive ambassadors, or as a duty vested with high executive discretion. The president has consequently the same authority to withhold, or to withdraw a commission, in the one case, as in the other, to receive or to decline receiving a foreign minister.

It follows that all the affirmative power in making treaties, in appointing to office, and in removing, is in the president alone, the advice and consent of the senate not authorising the several acts, but merely completing the right of the executive to perform these high functions himself.

The president of the United States, besides his civil duties, is the military commander in chief of the army and navy of the United States, at all times, and of the militia of the several states whenever the latter is called into the the field.

He is the representative of the constituencies of the states, under a peculiar modification, and for the purposes set forth in the constitution. He has no prerogative, which implies an inalienable and exclusive right or privilege, for his functions take the character of duties, and the states can legally, and under prescribed forms, not only modify those duties, but they can altogether destroy the office, at will.

As a rule, there is far more danger that the president of the United States will render the office less efficient than was intended, than that he will exercise an authority dangerous to the liberties of the country. Some of his powers perhaps, are too imitative, and are unnecessary; that of diminishing military officers, for instance. But it is a greater evil to attempt reducing them, except in conformity with the provisions of the constitution, than to endure them. Even these questionable points of power, have been seldom abused, and, as a whole, the history of the country shows ten instances of presidents' evading responsibility, to one of their abusing power. A recent case is that of the executive's assenting to an indirect law recognizing the independence of Texas, a measure that is purely diplomatick and international, and which, of course, ought to be regulated by treaty, and in no other manner. A step of this gravity, if referred to the proper authority, would have required the sanction of a two thirds vote in the senate, and consequently a deliberation and prudence that might do better justice, and possibly avoid a war.

On Equality

EQUALITY, in a social sense, may be divided into that of condition, and that of rights. Equality of condition is incompatible with civilization, and is found only to exist in those communities that are but slightly removed from the savage state. In practice, it can only mean a common misery.

Equality of rights is a peculiar feature of democracies. These rights are properly divided into civil and political, though even these definitions are not to be taken as absolute, or as literally exact.

Under the monarchies of the old world, there exist privileged classes, possessed of exclusive rights. For a long period the nobles were exempted from taxes, and many other charges, advantages that are still enjoyed by them, in certain countries. In England, even, the nobles are entitled to hereditary advantages that are denied to those who are of inferior birth. All these distinctions are done away with in principle, in countries where there exists a professed equality of rights, though there is probably no community that does not make some distinctions between the political privileges of men. If this be true, there is strictly no equality of political rights, any where, although there may be, and is, a nearer approach to an equality of civil rights.

By political rights we understand, the suffrage, eligibility to office, and a condition of things that admits of no distinction between men, unless on principles that are common to all. Thus, though a man is not qualified to vote until he has reached the age of twenty-one, the regulation does not effect political equality, since all are equally subject to the rule, and all become electors on attaining the same age.

With an equality of civil rights, all men are equal before the law; all classes of the community being liable equally to taxation, military service, jury duties, and to the other impositions attendant on civilization, and no one being exempted from its control, except on general rules, which are dependent on the good of all, instead of the exemption's belonging to the immunities of individuals, estates, or families. An equality of civil rights may be briefly defined to be an absence of privileges.

The distinction between the equality of civil and of political rights is material, one implying mere equality before the administration of the law, the other, equality in the power to frame it.

An equality of civil rights is never absolute, but we are to understand by the term, such an equality only, as is compatible with general justice and the relations between the different members of families. Thus, women nowhere possess precisely the same rights as men, or men the same rights as women. The wife, usually, can neither sue nor be sued, while the husband, except in particular cases, is made liable to all legal claims on account of the wife. Minors are deprived of many of their civil rights, or, it would be better to say, do not attain them, until they reach a period of life that has been arbitrarily fixed, and which varies in different countries, according to their several policies.

Neither is equality of political rights ever absolute. In those countries where the suffrage is said to be universal, exceptions exist, that arise from the necessity of things, or from that controlling policy which can never be safely lost sight of in the management of human affairs. The interests of women being thought to be so identified with those of their male relatives as to become, in a great degree, inseparable, females are, almost generally, excluded from the possession of political rights. There can be no doubt that society is greatly the gainer, by thus excluding one half its members, and the half that is best adapted to give a tone to its domestic happiness, from the strife of parties, and the fierce struggles of political controversies. Men are also excluded from political rights previously to having attained the age prescribed by law. Paupers, those who have no fixed abodes, and aliens in law, though their lives may have been principally passed in the country, are also excluded from the enjoyment of political rights, every where. Thus birth-right is almost universally made a source of advantage. These exceptions, however, do not very materially affect the principle of political equality, since the rules are general, and have been made solely with a reference to the good of society, or to render the laws less liable to abuses in practice.

It follows, that equality, whether considered in connection with our civil or political rights, must not be taken as a general and absolute condition of society, but as such an equality as depends on principles that are equitable, and which are suited to the actual wants of men.

On American Equality

THE equality of the United States is no more absolute, than that of any other country. There may be less inequality in this nation than in most others, but inequality exists, and, in some respects, with stronger features than it is usual to meet with in the rest of christendom.

The rights of property being an indispensable condition of civilization, and its quiet possession every where guarantied, equality of condition is rendered impossible. One man must labor, while another may live luxuriously on his means; one has leisure and opportunity to cultivate his tastes, to increase his information, and to refine his habits, while another is compelled to toil, that he may live. One is reduced to serve, while another commands, and, of course, there can be no equality in their social conditions.

The justice and relative advantage of these differencies, as well as their several duties, will be elsewhere considered.

By the inequality of civil and political rights that exists in certain parts of the Union, and the great equality that exists in others, we see the necessity of referring the true character of the institutions to those of the states, without a just understanding of which, it is impossible to obtain any general and accurate ideas of the real polity of the country.

The same general exceptions to civil and political equality, that are found in other free countries, exist in this, though under laws peculiar to ourselves. Women and minors are excluded from the suffrage, and from maintaining suits at law, under the usual provisions, here as well as elsewhere. None but natives of the country can fill many of the higher offices, and paupers, felons and all those who have not fixed residences, are also excluded from the suffrage. In a few of the states property is made the test of political rights, and, in nearly half of them, a large portion of the inhabitants, who are of a different race from the original European occupants of the soil, are entirely excluded from all political, and from many of the civil rights, that are enjoyed by those who are deemed citizens. A slave can neither choose, nor be chosen to office, nor, in most of the states, can even a free man, unless a white man. A slave can neither sue nor be sued; he can not hold property, real or personal, nor can he, in many of the states be a witness in any suit, civil or criminal.

It follows from these facts, that absolute equality of condition, of political rights, or of civil rights, does not exist in the United States, though they all exist in a much greater degree in some states than in others, and in some of the states, perhaps, to as great a degree as is practicable. In what are usually called the free states of America, or those in which domestic slavery is abolished, there is to be found as much equality in every respect as comports with safety, civilization and the rights of property. This is also true, as respects the white population, in those states in which domestic slavery does exist; though the number of the bond is in a large proportion to that of the free.

As the tendency of the institutions of America is to the right, we learn in these truths, the power of facts, every question of politics being strictly a question of practice. They who fancy it possible to frame the institutions of a country, on the pure principles of abstract justice, as these principles exist in theories, know little of human nature, or of the restraints that are necessary to society. Abuses assail us in a thousand forms, and it is hopeless to aspire to any condition of humanity, approaching perfection. The very necessity of a government at all, arises from the impossibility of controlling the passions by any other means than that of force.

The celebrated proposition contained in the declaration of independence is not to be understood literally. All men are not 'created equal,' in a physical, or even in a moral sense, unless we limit the signification to one of political rights. This much is true, since human institutions are a human invention, with which nature has had no connection. Men are not born equals, physically, since one has a good constitution, another a bad; one is handsome, another ugly; one white, another black. Neither are men born equals morally, one possessing genius, or a natural aptitude, while his brother is an idiot. As regards all human institutions men are born equal, no sophistry being able to prove that nature intended one should inherit power and wealth, another slavery and want. Still artificial inequalities are the inevitable consequences of artificial ordinances, and in founding a new governing principle for the social compact, the American legislators instituted new modes of difference.

The very existence of government at all, infers inequality. The citizen who is preferred to office becomes the superior of those who are not, so long as he is the repository of power, and the child inherits the wealth of the parent as a controlling law of society. All that the great American proposition, therefore, can mean, is to set up new and juster notions of natural rights than those which existed previously, by asserting, in substance, that God has not instituted political inequalities, as was pretended by the advocates of the Jus Divinum, and that men possessed a full and natural authority to form such social institutions as best suited their necessities.

There are numerous instances in which the social inequality of America may do violence to our notions of abstract justice, but the compromise of interests under which all civilized society must exist, renders this unavoidable. Great principles seldom escape working injustice in particular things, and this so much the more, in establishing the relations of a community, for in them many great, and frequently conflicting principles enter, to maintain the more essential features of which sacrifices of parts become necessary. If we would have civilization and the exertion indispensable to its success, we must have property; if we have property, we must have its rights; if we have the rights of property, we must take those consequences of the rights of property which are inseparable from the rights themselves.

The equality of rights in America, therefore, after allowing for the striking exception of domestic slavery, is only a greater extension of the principle than common, while there is no such thing as an equality of condition. All that can be said of the first, is that it has been carried as far as a prudent discretion will at all allow, and of the last, that the inequality is the simple result of civilization, unaided by any of those factitious plans that have been elsewhere devised in order to augment the power of the strong, and to enfeeble the weak.

Equality is no where laid down as a governing principle of the institutions of the United States, neither the word, nor any inference that can be fairly deduced from its meaning, occurring in the constitution. As respects the states, themselves, the professions of an equality of rights are more clear, and slavery excepted, the intention in all their governments is to maintain it, as far as practicable, though equality of condition is no where mentioned, all political economists knowing that it is unattainable, if, indeed, it be desirable. Desirable in practice, it can hardly be, since the result would be to force all down to the level of the lowest.

All that a good government aims at, therefore, is to add no unnecessary and artificial aid to the force of its own unavoidable consequences, and to abstain from fortifying and accumulating social inequality as a means of increasing political inequalities.

On Liberty

LIBERTY, like equality is a word more used than understood. Perfect and absolute liberty is as incompatible with the existence of society, as equality of condition. It is impracticable in a state of nature even, since, without the protection of the law, the strong would oppress and enslave the weak. We are then to understand by liberty, merely such a state of the social compact as permits the members of a community to lay no more restraints on themselves, than are required by their real necessities, and obvious interests. To this definition may be added, that it is a requisite of liberty, that the body of a nation should retain the power to modify its institutions, as circumstances shall require.

The natural disposition of all men being to enjoy a perfect freedom of action, it is a common error to suppose that the nation which possesses the mildest laws, or laws that impose the least personal restraints, is the freest. This opinion is untenable, since the power that concedes this freedom of action, can recall it. Unless it is lodged in the body of the community itself, there is, therefore, no pledge for the continuance of such a liberty. A familiar, supposititious case will render this truth more obvious.

A slave holder in Virginia is the master of two slaves: to one he grants his liberty, with the means to go to a town in a free state. The other accompanies his old associate clandestinely. In this town, they engage their services voluntarily, to a common master, who assigns to them equal shares in the same labor, paying them the same wages. In time, the master learns their situation, but, being an indulgent man, he allows the slave to retain his present situation. In all material things, these brothers are equal; they labor together, receive the same wages, and eat of the same food. Yet one is bond, and the other free, since it is in the power of the master, or of his heir, or of his assignee, at any time, to reclaim the services of the one who was not legally manumitted, and reduce him again to the condition of slavery. One of these brothers is the master of his own acts, while the other, though temporarily enjoying the same privileges, holds them subject to the will of a superior.

This is an all important distinction in the consideration of political liberty, since the circumstances of no two countries are precisely the same, and all municipal regulations ought to have direct reference to the actual condition of a community. It follows, that no country can properly be deemed free, unless the body of the nation possess, in the last resort, the legal power to frame its laws according to its wants. This power must also abide in the nation, or it becomes merely an historical fact, for he that was once free is not necessarily free always, any more than he that was once happy, is to consider himself happy in perpetuity.

This definition of liberty is new to the world, for a government founded on such principles is a novelty. Hitherto, a nation has been deemed free, whose people were possessed of a certain amount of franchises, without any reference to the general repository of power. Such a nation may not be absolutely enslaved, but it can scarcely be considered in possession of an affirmative political liberty, since it is not the master of its own fortunes.

Having settled what is the foundation of liberty, it remains to be seen by what process a people can exercise this authority over themselves. The usual course is to refer all matters of choice to the decision of majorities. The common axiom of democracies, however, which says that 'the majority must rule,' is to be received with many limitations. Were the majority of a country to rule without restraint, it is probable as much injustice and oppression would follow, as are found under the dominion of one. It belongs to the nature of men to arrange themselves in parties, to lose sight of truth and justice in partizanship and prejudice, to mistake their own impulses for that which is proper, and to do wrong because they are indisposed to seek the right. Were it wise to trust power, unreservedly, to majorities, all fundamental and controlling laws would be unnecessary, since they might, as occasion required, emanate from the will of numbers. Constitutions would be useless.

The majority rules in prescribed cases, and in no other. It elects to office, it enacts ordinary laws, subject however to the restrictions of the constitution, and it decides most of the questions that arise in the primitive meetings of the people; questions that do not usually effect any of the principal interests of life.

The majority does not rule in settling fundamental laws, under the constitution; or when it does rule in such cases, it is with particular checks produced by time and new combinations; it does not pass judgment in trials at law, or under impeachment, and it is impotent in many matters touching vested rights. In the state of New York, the majority is impotent, in granting corporations, and in appropriating money for local purposes.

Though majorities often decide wrong, it is believed that they are less liable to do so than minorities. There can be no question that the educated and affluent classes of a country, are more capable of coming to wise and intelligent decisions in affairs of state, than the mass of a population. Their wealth and leisure afford them opportunities for observation and comparison, while their general information and greater knowledge of character, enable them to judge more accurately of men and measures. That these opportunities are not properly used, is owing to the unceasing desire of men to turn their advantages to their own particular benefit, and to their passions. All history proves, when power is the sole possession of a few, that it is perverted to their sole advantage, the public suffering in order that their rulers may prosper. The same nature which imposes the necessity of governments at all, seems to point out the expediency of confiding its control, in the last resort, to the body of the nation, as the only lasting protection against gross abuses.

We do not adopt the popular polity because it is perfect, but because it is less imperfect than any other. As man, by his nature, is liable to err, it is vain to expect an infallible whole that is composed of fallible parts. The government that emanates from a single will, supposing that will to be pure, enlightened, impartial, just and consistent, would be the best in the world, were it attainable for men. Such is the government of the universe, the result of which is perfect harmony. As no man is without spot in his justice, as no man has infinite wisdom, or infinite mercy, we are driven to take refuge in the opposite extreme, or in a government of many.

It is common for the advocates of monarchy and aristocracy to deride the opinions of the mass, as no more than the impulses of ignorance and prejudices. While experience unhappily shows that this charge has too much truth, it also shows that the educated and few form no exemption to the common rule of humanity. The most intelligent men of every country in which there is liberty of thought and action, yielding to their interests or their passions, are always found taking the opposite extremes of contested questions, thus triumphantly refuting an arrogant proposition, that of the exclusive fitness of the few to govern, by an unanswerable fact. The minority of a country is never known to agree, except in its efforts to reduce and oppress the majority. Were this not so, parties would be unknown in all countries but democracies, whereas the factions of aristocracies have been among the fiercest and least governable of any recorded in history.

Although real political liberty can have but one character, that of a popular base, the world contains many modifications of governments that are, more or less, worthy to be termed free. In most of these states, however, the liberties of the mass, are of the negative character of franchises, which franchises are not power of themselves, but merely an exemption from the abuses of power. Perhaps no state exists, in which the people, either by usage, or by direct concessions from the source of authority, do not possess some of these franchises; for, if there is no such thing, in practice, as perfect and absolute liberty, neither is there any such thing, in practice, as total and unmitigated slavery. In the one case, nature has rendered man incapable of enjoying freedom without restraint, and in the other, incapable of submitting, entirely without resistance, to oppression. The harshest despots are compelled to acknowledge the immutable principles of eternal justice, affecting necessity and the love of right, for their most ruthless deeds.

England is a country in which the franchises of the subject are more than usually numerous. Among the most conspicuous of these are the right of trial by jury, and that of the *habeas corpus*. Of the former it is unnecessary to speak, but as the latter is a phrase that may be unintelligible to many, it may be well to explain it.

The literal signification of *Habeas Corpus* * is, 'thou may'st have the body.' In arbitrary governments, it is much the usage to oppress men, under the pretence of justice, by causing them to be arrested on false, or trivial charges, and of subjecting them to long and vexatious imprisonments, by protracting, or altogether evading the day of trial. The issue of a writ of *Habeas Corpus*, is an order to bring the accused before an impartial and independent judge, who examines into the charge, and who orders the prisoner to be set at liberty, unless there be sufficient legal ground for his detention.

This provision of the English law has been wisely retained in our system, for without some such regulation, it would be almost as easy to detain a citizen unjustly, under

---

* '*Habeas*,' second person singular, present tense, subjunctive mood, of the verb '*Habere*,' to have; '*Corpus*,' a noun, signifying 'body.'

a popular government, as to detain the subject of a monarchy; the difference in favor of the first, consisting only in the greater responsibility of its functionaries.

By comparing the privileges of the *Habeas Corpus*, where it exists alone, and as a franchise, with those of the citizen who enjoys it merely as a provision of his own, against the abuses of ordinances that he had a voice in framing, we learn the essential difference between real liberty and franchises. The Englishman can appeal to a tribunal, against the abuse of an existing law, but if the law be not with him, he has no power to evade it, however unjust, or oppressive. The American has the same appeal against the abuse of a law, with the additional power to vote for its repeal, should the law itself be vicious. The one profits by a franchise to liberate his person only, submitting to his imprisonment however, if legality has been respected; while the other, in addition to this privilege, has a voice in getting rid of the obnoxious law, itself, and in preventing a recurrence of the wrong.

Some countries have the profession of possessing a government of the people, because an ancient dynasty has been set aside in a revolution, and a new one seated on the throne, either directly by the people, or by a combination that has been made to assume the character of a popular decision. Admitting that a people actually had an agency in framing such a system, and in naming their ruler, they cannot claim to be free, since they have parted with the power they did actually possess. No proposition can be clearer than that he who has given away a thing is no longer its master.

Of this nature is the present government of France. In that country the ancient dynasty has been set aside by a combination of leaders, through the agency of a few active spirits among the mass, and a prince put upon the throne, who is virtually invested with all the authority of his predecessor. Still, as the right of the last sovereign is clearly derived from a revolution, which has been made to assume the appearance of popular will, his government is termed a government of the people. This is a fallacy that can deceive no one of the smallest reflection. Such a system may be the best that France can now receive, but it is a mystification to call it by any other than its proper name. It is not a government of consultation, but one of pure force as respects a vast majority of Frenchmen.

A good deal of the same objection lies against the government of Great Britain, which, though freer in practice than of France, is not based on a really free system. It may be said that both these governments are as free as comports with discretion, as indeed may be said of Turkey, since men get to be disqualified for the possession of any advantage in time; but such an admission is only an avowal of unfitness, and not a proof of enjoyment.

It is usual to maintain, that in democracies the tyranny of majorities is a greater evil than the oppression of minorities in narrow systems. Although this evil is exaggerated, since the laws being equal in their action it is not easy to oppress the few without oppressing all, it undeniably is the weak side of a popular government. To guard against this, we have framed constitutions, which point out the cases in which the majority shall decide, limiting their power, and bringing that they do possess within the circle of certain general and just principles. It will be elsewhere shown that it is a great mistake for the American citizen to take sides with the public, in doubtful cases affecting the rights of individuals, as this is the precise form in which oppression is most likely to exhibit itself in a popular government.

Although it is true, that no genuine liberty can exist without being based on popular authority in the last resort, it is equally true that it can not exist when thus based, without many restraints on the power of the mass. These restraints are necessarily various and numerous. A familiar example will show their action. The majority of the people of a state might be in debt to its minority. Were the power of the former unrestrained, circumstances might arise in which they would declare depreciated bank notes a legal tender, and thus clear themselves of their liabilities, at the expense of their creditors. To prevent this, the constitution orders that nothing shall be made a legal tender but the precious metals, thus limiting the power of majorities in a way that the government is not limited in absolute monarchies, in which paper is often made to possess the value of gold and silver.

Liberty therefore may be defined to be a controlling authority that resides in the body of a nation, but so restrained as only to be exercised on certain general principles that shall do as little violence to natural justice, as is compatible with the peace and security of society.

On the Advantages of a Monarchy

THE monarchical form of government has the advantages of energy for external purposes, as well as of simplicity in execution. It is prompt and efficient in attack. Its legislation is ready, emanating from a single will, and it has the means of respecting treaties with more fidelity than other systems.

As laws are framed on general principles, they sometimes work evil in particular cases, and in a government of the will, the remedy is applied with more facility than in a government of law.

In a monarchy, men are ruled without their own agency, and as their time is not required for the supervision or choice of the public agents, or the enactment of laws, their attention may be exclusively given to their personal interest. Could this advantage be enjoyed without the abuses of such a state of things, it would alone suffice to render this form of government preferable to all others, since contact with the affairs of state is one of the most corrupting of the influences to which men are exposed.

As a monarchy recedes from absolutism, and takes the character of constitutionality, it looses these advantages to a certain extent, assuming more of those of legality.

On the Advantages of an Aristocracy

THE aristocratical form of government, though in an unmitigated form one of the worst known, has many advantages when tempered by franchises. This latter is the real polity of Great Britain, though it is under the pretence of a monarchy. No government, however, can properly be called a monarchy, in which the monarch does not form a distinct and independent portion of the state. The king of England, by the theory of the constitution, is supposed to hold a balance between the lords and the commons, whereas he, in truth, may be said merely to hold a casting vote between the several factions of the aristocracy, when the forces of these factions neutralize each other.

Aristocracies have a facility in combining measures for their interests that is not enjoyed by democracies. The power being in the hands of a few, these few can act with a despatch and energy, which, though unequaled by those of a monarchy, commonly have the material advantage of better agents. In an aristocracy, influence among the aristocrats themselves depending chiefly on the manly qualities, history shows us that the public agents are usually more chosen for their services than in a monarchy, where the favor of the prince is the chief requisite for success; it may therefore be assumed that the higher qualities of those who

fill the public trusts, in an aristocracy, more than neutralize
the greater concentration of a monarchy, and render it the
most efficient form of government, for the purpose of conquest and foreign policy, that is known. Aristocracy has an
absorbing quality, if such a term may be used, by which
the active and daring of conquered territories, are induced
to join the conquerors, in order to share in the advantages
of the system. Thus we find that almost all the countries
that have made extensive conquests over civilized people,
and who have long retained them, have been aristocracies.
We get examples of the facilities of aristocracies to extend
their influence, as well as to retain it, in Rome, England,
Venice, Florence and many other states.

An aristocracy is a combination of many powerful men,
for the purpose of maintaining and advancing their own
particular interests. It is consequently a concentration of
all the most effective parts of a community for a given
end; hence its energy, efficiency and success. Of all the
forms of government, it is the one best adapted to support
the system of metropolitan sway, since the most dangerous
of the dependants can be bribed and neutralized, by admitting them to a participation of power. By this means it is
rendered less offensive to human pride than the administration of one. The present relations between England and
Ireland, are a striking instance of what is meant.

An aristocracy, unless unusually narrow, is peculiarly
the government of the enterprising and the ambitious. High
honors are attainable, and jealousy of rewards is confined
to individuals, seldom effecting the state. The tendency of
the system, therefore, is to render the aristocrats bold, independent and manly, and to cause them to be distinguished
from the mass. In an age as advanced as ours, the leisure of
the higher classes of an aristocracy, enable them to cultivate
their minds and to improve their tastes. Hence aristocracies
are particularly favorable to knowledge and the arts, as
both grow under patronage.

It is necessary to distinguish, however, between a political and a merely social aristocracy. These remarks apply chiefly to the former, which alone has any connexion with government. The term aristocracy, in fact, applies properly to no other, though vulgar use has perverted its signification to all nobles, and even to the gentry of democracies.

Advantages of a Democracy

THE principal advantage of a democracy, is a general elevation in the character of the people. If few are raised to a very great height, few are depressed very low. As a consequence, the average of society is much more respectable than under any other form of government. The vulgar charge that the tendency of democracies is to levelling, meaning to drag all down to the level of the lowest, is singularly untrue, its real tendency being to elevate the depressed to a condition not unworthy of their manhood. In the absence of privileged orders, entails and distinctions, devised permanently to separate men into social castes, it is true none are great but those who become so by their acts, but, confining the remark to the upper classes of society, it would be much more true to say that democracy refuses to lend itself to unnatural and arbitrary distinctions, than to accuse it of a tendency to level those who have a just claim to be elevated. A denial of a favor, is not an invasion of a right.

Democracies are exempt from the military charges, both pecuniary and personal, that become necessary in governments in which the majority are subjects, since no force is required to repress those who, under other systems, are dangerous to the state, by their greater physical power.

As the success of democracies is mainly dependant on the intelligence of the people, the means of preserving the government are precisely those which most conduce to the happiness and social progress of man. Hence we find the state endeavoring to raise its citizens in the scale of being, the certain means of laying the broadest foundation of national prosperity. If the arts are advanced in aristocracies, through the taste of patrons, in democracies, though of slower growth, they will prosper as a consequence of general information; or as a superstructure reared on a wider and more solid foundation.

Democracies being, as nearly as possible, founded in natural justice, little violence is done to the sense of right by the institutions, and men have less occasion than usual, to resort to fallacies and false principles in cultivating the faculties. As a consequence, common sense is more encouraged, and the community is apt to entertain juster notions of all moral truths, than under systems that are necessarily sophisticated. Society is thus a gainer in the greater element of happiness, or in the right perception of the different relations between men and things.

Democracies being established for the common interests, and the publick agents being held in constant check by the people, their general tendency is to serve the whole community, and not small portions of it, as is the case in narrow governments. It is as rational to suppose that a hungry man will first help his neighbor to bread, when master of his own acts, as to suppose that any but those who feel themselves to be truly public servants, will first bethink themselves of the publick, when in situations of publick trust. In a government of one, that one and his parasites will be the first and best served; in a government of a few, the few; and in a government of many, the many. Thus the general tendency of democratical institutions is to equalize advantages, and to spread its blessings over the entire surface of society.

Democracies, other things being equal, are the cheapest form of government, since little money is lavished in representation, and they who have to pay the taxes, have also, directly or indirectly, a voice in imposing them.

Democracies are less liable to popular tumults than any other polities, because the people, having legal means in their power to redress wrongs, have little inducement to employ any other. The man who can right himself by a vote, will seldom resort to a musket. Grievances, moreover, are less frequent, the most corrupt representatives of a democratick constituency generally standing in awe of its censure.

As men in bodies usually defer to the right, unless acting under erroneous impression, or excited by sudden resentments, democracies pay more respect to abstract justice, in the management of their foreign concerns, than either aristocracies or monarchies, an appeal always lying against abuses, or violations of principle, to a popular sentiment, that, in the end, seldom fails to decide in favor of truth.

In democracies, with a due allowance for the workings of personal selfishness, it is usually a motive with those in places of trust, to consult the interests of the mass, there being little doubt, that in this system, the entire community has more regard paid to its wants and wishes, than in either of the two others.

On the Disadvantages of a Monarchy

A MONARCHY is liable to those abuses which follow favoritism, the servants of the prince avenging themselves for their homage to one, by oppressing the many.

A monarchy is the most expensive of all forms of government, the regal state requiring a costly parade, and he who depends on his own power to rule, must strengthen that power by bribing the active and enterprising whom he cannot intimidate. Thus the favorites of an absolute prince, in connection with the charges of himself and family, frequently cost the state as much as its necessary expenditures.

It is the policy of a monarchy to repress thought, a knowledge of human rights being always dangerous to absolute, or exclusive power. Thus the people of monarchies are divided into the extremes of society, the intermediate and happiest classes being usually small, and inclined to favor their superiors from apprehension of the brutal ignorance of those below them.

Monarchies are subjected to the wars and to the policies of family alliances, the feelings and passions of the prince exercising a malign influence on the affairs of the state.

In monarchies the people are required to maintain a military force sufficient to support the throne, the system always exacting that the subject should pay the troops that are kept on foot to hold him in subjection.

Truth is trammelled in a monarchy, the system dreading collision with a power so dangerous to all factitious and one-sided theories.

Monarchies, especially those in which the crown possesses a real and predominant power, discourage sincerity and frankness of character, substituting appearances for virtue, and flattery and deception for wholesome facts.

Women often exercise an improper influence, and this from an impure motive, in monarchies, history tracing even wars to the passions of an offended mistress.

The public money is diverted from legitimate objects, to those who support the personal views, passions, caprices, or enmities of the prince.

Monarchies are subject to all those abuses, which depend on an irresponsible administration of power, and an absence of publicity; abuses that oppress the majority for the benefit of a few, and which induce subserviency of character, frauds, flatteries and other similar vices.

If, in this age, monarchies exhibit these results of the

system in milder forms, than in other centuries, it is owing to the increasing influence of the people, who may control systems, though in a less degree, indirectly as well as directly.

On the Disadvantages of Aristocracy

ARISTOCRACY has, in common with monarchy, the evils of an expenditure that depends on representation, the state maintaining little less pomp under aristocrats, than under princes.

It is compelled to maintain itself against the physical superiority of numbers also, by military charges that involve heavy personal services, and large expenditures of money.

Being a government of the few, it is in the main, as a necessity of human selfishness, administered in the interests of the few.

The ruled are depressed in consequence of the elevation of their rulers. Information is kept within circumscribed limits, lest the mass should come to a knowledge of their force, for horses would not submit to be put in harness and made to toil for hard task-masters, did they know as much as men.

Aristocracies partaking of the irresponsible nature of corporations, are soulless, possessing neither the personal feelings that often temper even despotism, nor submitting to the human impulses of popular bodies. This is one of the worst features of an aristocracy, a system that has shown itself more ruthless than any other, though tempered by civilization, for aristocracy and barbarism cannot exist in common.

As there are many masters in an aristocracy, the exactions are proportionably heavy, and this the more so, as they who impose the burthens generally find the means to evade their payment: the apophthegm that 'it is better to have one tyrant than many,' applying peculiarly to aristocracies, and not to democracies, which cannot permanently tyrannize at all, without tyrannizing over those who rule.

Aristocracies have a natural tendency to wars and aggrandizement, which bring with them the inevitable penalties of taxes, injustice, demoralization and blood-shed. This charge has been brought against republicks generally, but a distinction should be made between a republick with an aristocratical base, and a republick with a democratical base, their characters being as dissimilar as those of any two forms of government known. Aristocracies, feeling less of the better impulses of man, are beyond their influence, while their means of combining are so great, that they oftener listen to their interests than to those sentiments of natural justice that in a greater or less degree always control masses.

Aristocracies usually favor those vices that spring from the love of money, which there is divine authority for believing to be 'the root of all evil.' In modern aristocracies, the controlling principle is property, an influence the most corrupting to which men submit, and which, when its ordinary temptations are found united to those of political patronage and power, is much too strong for human virtue. Direct bribery, therefore, has been found to be the bane of aristocracies, the influence of individuals supplying the place of merit, services and public virtue. In Rome this system was conducted so openly, that every man of note had his 'clients,' a term which then signified one who depended on the favor of another for the advancement of his interests, and even for the maintenance of his rights.

Aristocracies wound the sense of natural justice, and consequently unsettle principles, by placing men, altogether unworthy of trust, in high hereditary situations, a circumstance that not only offends morals, but sometimes, though possibly less often than is commonly imagined, inflicts serious injuries on a state.

On this point however, too much importance must not be attached to theories, for in the practice of states a regard is necessarily paid to certain indispensable principles, and the comparative merits of systems are to be established from their general tendencies, rather than from the accidental exceptions that may occasionally arise: the quality in the *personnel* of administrations depending quite as much on the general civilization of a nation, as on any other cause.

On the Disadvantages of Democracy

DEMOCRACIES are liable to popular impulses, which, necessarily arising from imperfect information, often work injustice from good motives. Tumults of the people are less apt to occur in democracies than under any other form of government, for, possessing the legal means of redressing themselves, there is less necessity to resort to force, but, public opinion, constituting, virtually, the power of the state, measures are more apt to be influenced by sudden mutations of sentiment, than under systems where the rulers have better opportunities and more leisure for examination. There is more feeling and less design in the movements of masses than in those of small bodies, except as design emanates from demagogues and political managers.

The efforts of the masses that are struggling to obtain their rights, in monarchies and aristocracies, however, are not to be imputed to democracy; in such cases, the people use their natural weapon, force, merely because they are denied any participation in the legal authority.

When democracies are small, these impulses frequently do

great injury to the public service, but in large states they are seldom of sufficient extent to produce results before there is time to feel the influence of reason. It is, therefore, one of the errors of politicians to imagine democracies more practicable in small than in large communities, an error that has probably arisen from the fact that, the ignorance of masses having hitherto put men at the mercy of the combinations of the affluent and intelligent, democracies have been permitted to exist only in countries insignificant by their wealth and numbers.

Large democracies, on the other hand, while less exposed to the principal evil of this form of government, than smaller, are unable to scrutinize and understand character with the severity and intelligence that are of so much importance in all representative governments, and consequently the people are peculiarly exposed to become the dupes of demagogues and political schemers, most of the crimes of democracies arising from the faults and designs of men of this character, rather than from the propensities of the people, who, having little temptation to do wrong, are seldom guilty of crimes except through ignorance.

Democracies are necessarily controlled by publick opinion, and failing of the means of obtaining power more honestly, the fraudulent and ambitious find a motive to mislead, and even to corrupt the common sentiment, to attain their ends. This is the greatest and most pervading danger of all large democracies, since it is sapping the foundations of society, by undermining its virtue. We see the effects of this baneful influence, in the openness and audacity with which men avow improper motives and improper acts, trusting to find support in a popular feeling, for while vicious influences are perhaps more admitted in other countries, than in America, in none are they so openly avowed.

It may also be urged against democracies, that, nothing being more corrupting than the management of human affairs, which are constantly demanding sacrifices of permanent principles to interests that are as constantly fluctuating, their people are exposed to assaults on their morals from this quarter, that the masses of other nations escape. It is probable, however, that this evil, while it ought properly to be enumerated as one of the disadvantages of the system, is more than counterbalanced by the main results, even on the score of morals.

The constant appeals to public opinion in a democracy, though excellent as a corrective of public vices, induce private hypocrisy, causing men to conceal their own convictions when opposed to those of the mass, the latter being seldom wholly right, or wholly wrong. A want of national manliness is a vice to be guarded against, for the man who would dare to resist a monarch, shrinks from opposing an entire community. That the latter is quite often wrong, however, is abundantly proved by the fact, that its own judgments fluctuate, as it reasons and thinks differently this year, or this month even, from what it reasoned and thought the last.

The tendency of democracies is, in all things, to mediocrity, since the tastes, knowledge and principles of the majority form the tribunal of appeal. This circumstance, while it certainly serves to elevate the average qualities of a nation, renders the introduction of a high standard difficult. Thus do we find in literature, the arts, architecture and in all acquired knowledge, a tendency in America to gravitate towards the common center in this, as in other things; lending a value and estimation to mediocrity that are not elsewhere given. It is fair to expect, however, that a foundation so broad, may in time sustain a superstructure of commensurate proportions, and that the influence of masses will in this, as in other interests, have a generally beneficial effect. Still it should not be forgotten that, with the exception of those works, of which, as they appeal to human sympathies or the practices of men, an intelligent public is the best judge, the mass of no community is qualified to decide the most correctly on any thing, which, in its nature, is above its reach.

It is a besetting vice of democracies to substitute publick opinion for law. This is the usual form in which masses of men exhibit their tyranny. When the majority of the entire community commits this fault it is a sore grievance, but when local bodies, influenced by local interests, pretend to style themselves the publick, they are assuming powers that properly belong to the whole body of the people, and to them only under constitutional limitations. No tyranny of one, nor any tyranny of the few, is worse than this. All attempts in the publick, therefore, to do that which the publick has no right to do, should be frowned upon as the precise form in which tyranny is the most apt to be displayed in a democracy.

Democracies, depending so much on popular opinion are more liable to be influenced to their injury, through their management of foreign and hostile nations, than other governments. Is is generally known that, in Europe, secret means are resorted to, to influence sentiment in this way, and we have witnessed in this country open appeals to the people, against the acts of their servants, in matters of foreign relations, made by foreign, not to say, hostile agents. Perhaps no stronger case can be cited of this weakness on the part of democracies, than is shown in this fact, for here we find men sufficiently audacious to build the hope of so far abusing opinion, as to persuade a people to act directly against their own dignity and interests.

The misleading of publick opinion in one way or another, is the parent of the principal disadvantages of a democracy, for in most instances it is first corrupting a community in order that it may be otherwise injured. Were it not for the counteracting influence of reason, which, in the end, seldom, perhaps never fails to assert its power, this defect would of itself, be sufficient to induce all discreet men to decide against this form of government. The greater the danger, the greater the necessity that all well-intentioned and right-minded citizens should be on their guard against its influence.

It would be hazardous, however, to impute all the peculiar faults of American character, to the institutions, the country existing under so many unusual influences. If the latter were overlooked, one might be induced to think frankness and sincerity of character were less encouraged by popular institutions than was formerly supposed, close observers affirming that these qualities are less frequent here, than in most other countries. When the general ease of society is remembered, there is unquestionably more deception of opinion practised than one would naturally expect, but this failing is properly to be imputed to causes that have no necessary connection with democratical institutions, though men defer to publick opinion, right or wrong, quite as submissively as they defer to princes. Although truths are not smothered altogether in democracies, they are often temporarily abandoned under this malign influence, unless there is a powerful motive to sustain them at the moment. While we see in our own democracy this manifest disposition to defer to the wrong, in matters that are not properly subject to the common sentiment, in deference to the popular will of the hour, there is a singular boldness in the use of personalities, as if men avenged themselves for the restraints of the one case by a licentiousness that is without hazard.

The base feelings of detraction and envy have more room for exhibition, and perhaps a stronger incentive in a democracy, than in other forms of government, in which the people get accustomed to personal deference by the artificial distinctions of the institutions. This is the reason that men become impatient of all superiority in a democracy, and manifest a wish to prefer those who affect a deference to the publick, rather than those who are worthy.

On Prejudice

PREJUDICE is the cause of most of the mistakes of bodies of men. It influences our conduct and warps our judgment, in politics, religion, habits, tastes and opinions. We confide in one statesman and oppose another, as often from unfounded antipathies, as from reason; religion is tainted with uncharitableness and hostilities, without examination; usages are condemned; tastes ridiculed, and we decide wrong, from the practice of submitting to a preconceived and an unfounded prejudice, the most active and the most pernicious of all the hostile agents of the human mind.

The migratory propensities of the American people, and the manner in which the country has been settled by immigrants from all parts of the christian world, have an effect in diminishing prejudices of a particular kind, though, in other respects, few nations are more bigotted or provincial in their notions. Innovations on the usages connected with the arts of life are made here with less difficulty than common, reason, interest and enterprise proving too strong for prejudice; but in morals, habits and tastes, few nations have less liberality to boast of, than this.

America owes most of its social prejudices to the exaggerated religious opinions of the different sects which were so instrumental in establishing the colonies. The quakers, or friends, proscribed the delightful and elevated accomplishment of music, as, indeed, did the puritans, with the exception of psalmody. The latter confined marriage ceremonies to the magistrates, lest religion should be brought into disrepute! Most of those innocent recreations which help the charities, and serve to meliorate manners, were also forbidden, until an unnatural and monastic austerity, with a caustic habit of censoriousness, got to be considered as the only outward signs of that religious hope, which is so peculiarly adapted to render us joyous and benevolent.

False and extravagant notions on the subject of manners, never fail to injure a sound morality, by mistaking the shadow for the substance. Positive vice is known by all, for happily, conscience and revelation have made us acquainted with the laws of virtue, but it is as indiscreet unnecessarily to enlarge the circle of sins, as it is to expose ourselves to temptations that experience has shown we are unable to resist.

The most obvious American prejudices, connected with morality, are the notions that prevail on the subject of mispending time. That time may be mispent is undeniable, and few are they who ought not to reproach themselves with this neglect, but the human mind needs relaxation and amusement, as well as the human body. These are to be sought in the different expedients of classes, each finding the most satisfaction in those indulgences that conform the nearest to their respective tastes. It is the proper duty of the legislator to endeavor to elevate these tastes, and not to prevent their indulgence. Those nations in which the cord of moral discipline, according to the dogmas of fanatics, has drawn the tightest, usually exhibit the gravest scenes of depravity, on the part of those who break loose from restraints so ill judged and unnatural. On the other hand, the lower classes of society, in nations where amusements are tolerated, are commonly remarkable for possessing some of the tastes that denote cultivation and refinement. Thus do we find in catholic countries, that the men who in protestant nations, would pass their leisure in the coarsest indulgences, frequent operas and theatrical representations, classes of amusements which, well conducted, may be made powerful auxiliaries of virtue, and which generally have a tendency to improve the tastes. It is to be remarked that these exhibitions themselves are usually less gross, and more intellectual in catholic, than in protestant countries, a result of this improvement in manners.

The condition of this country is peculiar, and requires greater exertions than common, in extricating the mind from prejudices. The intimate connexion between popular opinion and positive law is one reason, since under a union so close there is danger that the latter may be colored by motives that have no sufficient foundation in justice. It is vain to boast of liberty, if the ordinances of society are to receive the impression of sectarianism, or of a provincial and narrow morality.

Another motive peculiar to the country, for freeing the mind from prejudice, is the mixed character of the population. Natives of different sections of the United States, and of various parts of Europe are brought in close contact, and without a disposition to bear with each other's habits, association becomes unpleasant, and enmities are engendered. The main result is to liberalize the mind, beyond a question, yet we see neighborhoods, in which oppressive intolerance is manifested by the greater number, for the time being, to the habits of the less. This is a sore grievance, more especially, when, as is quite frequently the case, the minority happen to be in possession of usages that mark the highest stage of civilization. It ought never to be forgotten, therefore, that every citizen is entitled to indulge without comment, or persecution, in all his customs and practices that are lawful and moral. Neither is morality to be regulated by the prejudices of sects, or social classes, but it is to be left strictly to the control of the laws, divine and human. To assume the contrary is to make prejudice, and prejudice of a local origin too, more imperious than the institutions. The justice, not to say necessity of these liberal concessions, is rendered more apparent when we remember that the parties meet as emigrants on what may be termed neutral territory, for it would be the height of presumption for the native of New York, for instance, to insist on his own peculiar customs, customs that other portions of the country perhaps repudiate, within the territory of New England, in opposition not only to the wishes of many of their brother emigrants, but to those of the natives themselves.

On Station

STATION may be divided into that which is political, or publick, and that which is social, or private. In monarchies and aristocracies the two are found united, since the higher classes, as a matter of course, monopolize all the offices of consideration; but, in democracies, there is not, nor is it proper that there should be, any intimate connexion between them.

Political, or publick station, is that which is derived from office, and, in a democracy, must embrace men of very different degrees of leisure, refinement, habits and knowledge. This is characteristick of the institutions, which, under a popular government, confer on political station more power than rank, since the latter is expressly avoided in this system.

Social station is that which one possesses in the ordinary associations, and is dependent on birth, education, personal qualities, property, tastes, habits, and, in some instances, on caprice, or fashion. Although the latter undeniably is sometimes admitted to control social station, it generally depends, however, on the other considerations named.

Social station, in the main, is a consequence of property. So long as there is civilization there must be the rights of property, and so long as there are the rights of property, their obvious consequences must follow. All that democracies legitimately attempt is to prevent the advantages which accompany social station from accumulating rights that do not properly belong to the condition, which is effected by pronouncing that it shall have no factitious political aids.

They who have reasoned ignorantly, or who have aimed at effecting their personal ends by flattering the popular feeling, have boldly affirmed that 'one man is as good as another;' a maxim that is true in neither nature, revealed morals, nor political theory.

That one man is not as good as another in natural qualities, is proved on the testimony of our senses. One man is stronger than another; he is handsomer, taller, swifter, wiser, or braver, than all his fellows. In short the physical and moral qualities are unequally distributed, and, as a necessary consequence, in none of them, can one man be justly said to be as good as another. Perhaps no two human beings can be found so precisely equal in every thing, that one shall not be pronounced the superior of the other; which, of course, establishes the fact that there is no natural equality.

The advocates of exclusive political privileges reason on this circumstance by assuming, that as nature has made differences between men, those institutions which create political orders, are no more than carrying out the great designs of providence. The error of their argument is in supposing it a confirmation of the designs of nature to attempt to supplant her, for, while the latter has rendered men unequal, it is not from male to male, according to the order of primogeniture, as is usually established by human ordinances. In order not to interfere with the inequality of nature, her laws must be left to their own operations, which is just what is done in democracies, after a proper attention has been paid to the peace of society, by protecting the weak against the strong.

That one man is not deemed as good as another in the grand moral system of providence, is revealed to us in Holy Writ, by the scheme of future rewards and punishments, as well as by the whole history of those whom God has favored in this world, for their piety, or punished for their rebellion.

As compared with perfect holiness, all men are frail; but, as compared with each other, we are throughout the whole of sacred history made to see, that, in a moral sense, one man is not as good as another. The evil doer is punished, while they who are distinguished for their qualities and acts, are intended to be preferred.

The absolute moral and physical equality that are inferred by the maxim, that 'one man is as good as another,' would at once do away with the elections, since a lottery would be both simpler, easier and cheaper than the present mode of selecting representatives. Men, in such a case, would draw lots for office, as they are now drawn for juries. Choice supposes a preference, and preference inequality of merit, or of fitness.

We are then to discard all visionary theories on this head, and look at things as they are. All that the most popular institutions attempt, is to prohibit that one *race* of men shall be made better than another by law, from father to son, which would be defeating the intentions of providence, creating a superiority that exists in neither physical nor moral nature, and substituting a political scheme for the will of God and the force of things.

As a principle, one man is as good as another in rights. Such is the extent of the most liberal institutions of this country, and this provision is not general. The slave is not as good as his owner, even in rights. But in those states where slavery does not exist, all men have essentially the same rights, an equality, which, so far from establishing that 'one man is as good as another,' in a social sense, is the very means of producing the inequality of condition that actually exists. By possessing the same rights to exercise their respective faculties, the active and frugal become more wealthy than the idle and dissolute; the wise and gifted more trusted than the silly and ignorant; the polished and refined more respected and sought, than the rude and vulgar.

In most countries, birth is a principal source of social distinction, society being divided into castes, the noble having an hereditary claim to be the superior of the plebeian. This is an unwise and an arbitrary distinction that has led to most of the social diseases of the old world, and from which America is happily exempt. But great care must be had in construing the principles which have led to this great change, for America is the first important country of modern times, in which such positive distinctions have been destroyed.

Still some legal differences, and more social advantages, are produced by birth, even in America. The child inherits the property, and a portion of the consideration of the parent. Without the first of these privileges, men would not exert themselves to acquire more property than would suffice for their own personal necessities, parental affection being one of the most powerful incentives to industry. Without such an inducement, then, it would follow that civilization would become stationary, or, it would recede; the incentives of individuality and of the affections, being absolutely necessary to impel men to endure the labor and privations that alone can advance it.

The hereditary consideration of the child, so long as it is kept within due bounds, by being confined to a natural sentiment, is also productive of good, since no more inducement to great and glorious deeds can offer, than the deeply seated interest that man takes in his posterity. All that reason and justice require is effected, by setting bounds to such advantages, in denying hereditary claims to trusts and power; but evil would be the day, and ominous the symptom, when a people shall deny that any portion of the consideration of the ancestor is due to the descendant.

It is as vain to think of altogether setting aside sentiment and the affections, in regulating human affairs, as to imagine it possible to raise a nature, known to be erring and weak, to the level of perfection.

The Deity, in that terrible warning delivered from the mount, where he declares that he 'will visit the sins of the fathers upon the children, unto the third and fourth generation,' does no more than utter one of those sublime moral truths, which, in conformity with his divine providence, pervade nature. It is merely an announcement of a principle that cannot safely be separated from justice, and one that is closely connected with all the purest motives and highest aspirations of man.

There would be a manifest injustice in visiting the offence of the criminal on his nearest of kin, by making the innocent man participate in the disgrace of a guilty relative, as is notoriously done most, by those most disposed to rail at reflected renown, and not to allow of the same participation in the glory. Both depend upon a sentiment deeper than human laws, and have been established for purposes so evidently useful as to require no explanation. All that is demanded of us, is to have a care that this sentiment do not degenerate to a prejudice, and that, in the one case, we do not visit the innocent too severely, or, in the other, exalt the unworthy beyond the bounds of prudence.

It is a natural consequence of the rights of property and of the sentiment named, that birth should produce some advantages, in a social sense, even in the most democratical of the American communities. The son imbibes a portion of the intelligence, refinement and habits of the father, and he shares in his associations. These must be enumerated as the legitimate advantages of birth, and without invading the private arrangements of families and individuals, and establishing a perfect community of education, they are unavoidable. Men of the same habits, the same degree of cultivation and refinement, the same opinions, naturally associate together, in every class of life. The day laborer will not mingle with the slave; the skilful mechanic feels his superiority over the mere laborer, claims higher wages and has a pride in his craft; the man in trade justly fancies that his habits elevate him above the mechanic, so far as social position is concerned, and the man of refinement, with his education, tastes and sentiments, is superior to all. Idle declamation on these points, does not impair the force of things, and life is a series of facts. These inequalities of condition, of manners, of mental cultivation must exist, unless it be intended to reduce all to a common level of ignorance and vulgarity, which would be virtually to return to a condition of barbarism.

The result of these undeniable facts, is the inequalities of social station, in America, as elsewhere, though it is an inequality that exists without any more arbitrary distinctions than are indispensably connected with the maintenance of civilization. In a social sense, there are orders here, as in all other countries, but the classes run into each other more easily, the lines of separation are less strongly drawn, and their shadows are more intimately blended.

This social inequality of America is an unavoidable result of the institutions, though nowhere proclaimed in them, the different constitutions maintaining a profound silence on the subject, they who framed them probably knowing that it is as much a consequence of civilized society, as breathing is a vital function of animal life.

On the Duties of Station

THE duties of station are divided into those of political or public station, and those of social, or private station. They are not necessarily connected, and shall be considered separately.

ON THE DUTIES OF
PUBLICK OR POLITICAL STATION

By the duties of publick station, we understand those of the private citizen, as well as those of the citizen who fills a publick trust. The first lie at the root of the social compact, and are entitled to be first enumerated.

On the manner in which the publick duties of the private citizen are discharged, in a really free government, depend the results of the institutions. If the citizen is careless of his duties, regardless of his rights, and indifferent to the common weal, it is not difficult to foresee the triumph of abuses, peculation and frauds. It is as unreasonable to suppose that the private servant who is not overlooked, will be faithful to his master, as to suppose that the publick servant who is not watched, will be true to his trusts. In both cases a steady, reasoning, but vigilant superintendance is necessary to the good of all concerned; to the agent by removing the temptation to err, and to the principal by securing an active attention to his interests.

The American citizens are possessed of the highest political privileges that can fall to the lot of the body of any community; that of self-government. On the discreet use of this great power, depends the true character of the institutions. It is, consequently, an imperious duty of every elector to take care and employ none but the honest and intelligent, in situations of high trust.

Every position in life has its peculiar dangers, men erring more from an inability to resist temptation, than from any morbid inward impulses to do wrong without an inducement. The peculiar danger of a democracy, arises from the arts of demagogues. It is a safe rule, the safest of all, to confide only in those men for publick trusts, in whom the citizen can best confide in private life. There is no quality that more entirely pervades the moral system than probity.

We often err on certain points, each man having a besetting sin, but honesty colors a whole character. He who in private is honest, frank, above hypocricy and double-dealing, will carry those qualities with him into publick, and may be confided in; while he who is the reverse, is, inherently, a knave.

The elector who gives his vote for one whom he is persuaded on good grounds is dishonest in his motives, abuses the most sacred of his public duties. It is true, that party violence, personal malice and love of gossip, frequently cause upright men to be distrusted, and that great care is necessary to guard against slander, the commonest of human crimes, and a besetting vice of a democracy; but the connection between the constituent and the representative is usually so close, that the former, by resorting to proper means, can commonly learn the truth. Let it be repeated, then, that the elector who gives his vote, on any grounds, party or personal, to an unworthy candidate, violates a sacred publick duty, and is unfit to be a freeman.

Obedience to the laws, and a sacred regard to the rights of others, are imperative publick duties of the citizen. As he is a 'law-maker,' he should not be a 'law-breaker,' for he ought to be conscious that every departure from the established ordinances of society is an infraction of his rights. His power can only be maintained by the supremacy of the laws, as in monarchies, the authority of the king is asserted by obedience to his orders. The citizen in lending a cheerful assistance to the ministers of the law, on all occasions, is merely helping to maintain his own power. This feature in particular, distinguishes the citizen from the subject. The one rules, the other is ruled; one has a voice in framing the ordinances, and can be heard in his efforts to repeal them; the other has no choice but submission.

In Democracies there is a besetting disposition to make

publick opinion stronger than the law. This is the particular form in which tyranny exhibits itself in a popular government; for wherever there is power, there will be found a disposition to abuse it. Whoever opposes the interests, or wishes of the publick, however right in principle, or justifiable by circumstances, finds little sympathy; for, in a democracy, resisting the wishes of the many, is resisting the sovereign, in his caprices. Every good citizen is bound to separate this influence of his private feelings from his publick duties, and to take heed that, while pretending to be struggling for liberty, because contending for the advantage of the greatest number, he is not helping despotism. The most insinuating and dangerous form in which oppression can overshadow a community is that of popular sway. All the safeguards of liberty, in a democracy, have this in view, as, in monarchies, they are erected against the power of the crown.

The old political saying, that 'the people are their own worst enemies,' while false as a governing maxim, contains some truth. It is false to say that a people left to govern themselves, would oppress themselves, as monarchs and aristocrats, throughout all time, are known to oppress the ruled, but it is true to say, that the peculiar sins of a democracy must be sought for in the democratical character of the institutions. To pretend otherwise, would be to insist on perfection; for, in a state of society in which there is neither prince nor aristocrats, there must be faultlessness, or errors of a democratic origin, and of a democratic origin only. It is, therefore, a publick duty of the citizen to guard against all excesses of popular power, whether inflicted by mere opinion, or under the forms of law. In all his publick acts, he should watch himself, as under a government of another sort he would watch his rulers; or as vigilantly as he watches the servants of the community at home; for, though possessing the power in the last resort, it is not so absolutely an irresponsible power as it first seems, coming from God, and to be wielded on those convictions of right which God has implanted in our breasts, that we may know good from evil.

ON THE PRIVATE DUTIES OF STATION

The private duties of the citizen, as connected with social station, are founded chiefly on the relations between man and man, though others may be referred to a higher source, being derived directly from the relations between the creature and his creator.

A regard for the duties of private station, are indispensable to order, and to the intercourse between different members of society. So important have they always been deemed, that the inspired writers, from the Saviour through the greatest of his apostles down, have deemed them worthy of being placed in conspicuous characters, in their code of morals.

The first direct mandates of God, as delivered on Mount Sinai, were to impress the Jews with a sense of their duties to their Heavenly Father; the next to impress them with the first of their social duties, that of honor and obedience to their parents.

The fifth commandment, then, may be said to contain the first of our social duties. It is strictly one of station, for it enforces the obligation of the child to its parents. Nor is this all; the entire extent of the family relations are included in principle, since it cannot be supposed that those who precede our immediate parents, are excluded from the general deference that we owe to the greater experience, the love, and the care of our predecessors.

It is apparent throughout the code of christian morals, that a perfect reciprocity between the duties of social station is nowhere inferred. 'Nevertheless,' says St Paul, 'let every one of you in particular, so love his wife, even as himself; and the wife *see* that she *reverence* her husband.' There is an obligation of deference imposed on the wife, that is not imposed on the husband. 'Servants be obedient to them that are your masters according to the flesh, with fear and trembling, in singleness of heart, as unto Christ.' By these, and many similar mandates, we perceive that the private duties of station are constantly recognized, and commanded, by the apostles, as well as by the Saviour.

The old abuses of power, with the attendant reaction, have unsettled the publick mind, in many essential particulars, on this important point. Interested men have lent their aid to mislead the credulous and vain, until a confusion in the relations between the different members of society has arisen, that must, more or less, lead to confusion in society itself.

After the direct family relations, come the private duties that are generally connected with station, as between master and servant.

Whoever employs, with the right to command, is a master; and, whoever serves, with an obligation to obey, a servant. These are the broad signification of the two words, and, in this sense they are now used.

It is an imperative obligation on those who command, to be kind in language, however firm, and to use a due consideration in issuing their orders. The greater the duty of those, whose part it is to obey, to comply with all just and reasonable requisitions, or, in other words, to conform to the terms of their service, the greater is the duty of the master to see that he does not exact more than propriety will warrant. On the other hand, they who serve owe a respectful and decorous obedience, showing by their manner as well by their acts, they understand that without order and deference, the different social relations can never be suitably filled. So far from republican institutions making any difference in this respect, in favor of him who serves, they increase the moral duty to be respectful and assiduous, since service in such a case, is not the result of political causes, but a matter of convention, or bargain.

The relations between the master and the domestic servant, are peculiar, and are capable of being made of a very endearing and useful nature. The house servant, whether man or woman, fills a more honorable, because a much more confidential station, than the lower mechanic, or farm laborer. The domestics are intrusted with the care of the children of those they serve, have necessarily charge of much valuable property, and are, in a manner, intrusted with the secrets of the domestic economy. The upper servants of a considerable and well bred family, or of those who are accustomed to the station they fill, and have not been too suddenly elevated by the chances of life, are often persons of a good education, accustomed to accounts, and, in a measure, familiarized to the usages of polite life, since they see them daily practised before their eyes. Such persons invariably gain some of the refinement and tone of mind that marks the peculiar condition of their employers.

The rule of most civilized nations, is for the master to treat the servant as an humble friend. In more polished countries of Europe, the confidential domestic holds a high place in the household, and, after a long service, is commonly considered as an inferior member of the family.

It is a misfortune of America to admit so many of the dogmas of the country from which she is derived, while living in a state of society so very different. An attempt to treat and consider a domestic, as domestics are treated and considered in England, is unwise, and, in fact, impracticable. The English servant fares worse, in many particulars, than the servant of almost every other nation. France would be a better and a safer model, in this particular, the masters of France being usually much milder and more considerate than those of England, while the servants are altogether superior. The French servant is not as cleanly and thorough in his work, as the English servant, a difference in the habits of the country forbidding it; but he is generally more attached, better informed, more agreeable as a companion, quite as serviceable, the exception mentioned apart, and more faithful, honest and prudent. This is true of both sexes; the female domestics of France, while less tidy in household work than those of England or America, being altogether superior to both, in moral qualities, tastes, general usefulness and knowledge.

A beautiful instance of the effect of the duties of social station is before the eyes of the writer, even while he pens this paragraph; that of an aged woman, who passed her youth in the service of one family, ministering to the wants of three generations, and is now receiving the gratitude which long and patient toil has earned. On the one side is affection, delicacy, and attention to the wants of age; on the other a love little short of that of a mother's, softened by the respect that has always marked the life of one in whom a sense of the duties of social station has never been weakened. Nothing still makes this venerable servant more happy, than to be employed for those whom she has seen ushered into life, whom she first fondled on the knee, while these, again, mindful of her years and increasing infirmities, feel it a source of pleasure to anticipate her little wants, and to increase her comforts. The conditions of master and servant are those of co-relatives, and when they are properly understood they form additional ties to the charities and happiness of life. It is an unhappy effect of the unformed habits of society in this country, and of domestic slavery, that we are so much wanting in this beautiful feature in domestic economy.

The social duties of a gentleman are of a high order. The class to which he belongs is the natural repository of the manners, tastes, tone, and, to a certain extent, of the principles of a country. They who imagine this portion of the community useless, drones who consume without producing, have not studied society, or they have listened to the suggestions of personal envy, instead of consulting history and facts. If the laborer is indispensable to civilization, so is also the gentleman. While the one produces, the other directs his skill to those arts which raise the polished man above the barbarian. The last brings his knowledge and habits to bear upon industry, and, taking the least favorable view of his claims, the indulgence of his very luxuries encourages the skill that contributes to the comforts of the lowest.

Were society to be satisfied with a mere supply of the natural wants, there would be no civilization. The savage condition attains this much. All beyond it, notwithstanding, is so much progress made in the direction of the gentleman, and has been made either at the suggestions, or by the encouragement of those whose means have enabled, and whose tastes have induced them to buy. Knowledge is as necessary to the progress of a people as physical force, for, with our knowledge, the beasts of burthen who now toil for man, would soon compel man to toil for them. If the head is necessary to direct the body, so is the head of society, (the head in a social, if not in a political sense,) necessary to direct the body of society.

Any one may learn the usefulness of a body of enlightened men in a neighborhood, by tracing their influence on its civilization. Where many such are found, the arts are more advanced, and men learn to see that there are tastes more desirable than those of the mere animal. In such a neighborhood they acquire habits which contribute to their happiness by advancing their intellect, they learn the value of refinement in their intercourse, and obtain juster notions of the nature and of the real extent of their rights. He who would honor learning, and taste, and sentiment, and refinement of every sort, ought to respect its possessors, and, in all things but those which affect rights, defer to their superior advantages. This is the extent of the deference that is due from him who is not a gentleman, to him who is; but this much is due.

On the other hand, the social duties of an American

gentleman, in particular, require of him a tone of feeling and a line of conduct that are of the last importance to the country. One of the first of his obligations is to be a guardian of the liberties of his fellow citizens. It is peculiarly graceful in the American, whom the accidents of life have raised above the mass of the nation, to show himself conscious of his duties in this respect, by asserting at all times the true principles of government, avoiding, equally, the cant of demagogueism with the impracticable theories of visionaries, and the narrow and selfish dogmas of those who would limit power by castes. They who do not see and feel the importance of possessing a class of such men in a community, to give it tone, a high and far sighted policy, and lofty views in general, can know little of history and have not reflected on the inevitable consequences of admitted causes.

The danger to the institutions of denying to men of education their proper place in society, is derived from the certainty that no political system can long continue in which this violence is done to the natural rights of a class so powerful. It is as unjust to require that men of refinement and training should defer in their habits and associations to the notions of those who are their inferiors in these particulars, as it is to insist that political power should be the accompaniment of birth. All, who are in the least cultivated, know how irksome and oppressive is the close communion with ignorance and vulgarity, and the attempt to push into the ordinary associations, the principles of equality that do and ought to govern states in their political characters, is, virtually, an effort to subvert a just general maxim, by attaching to it impracticable consequences.

Whenever the enlightened, wealthy, and spirited of an affluent and great country, seriously conspire to subvert democratical institutions, their leisure, money, intelligence and means of combining, will be found too powerful for the ill-directed and conflicting efforts of the mass. It is therefore, all important, to enlist a portion of this class, at least, in the cause of freedom, since its power at all times renders it a dangerous enemy.

Liberality is peculiarly the quality of a gentleman. He is liberal in his attainments, opinions, practices and concessions. He asks for himself, no more than he is willing to concede to others. He feels that his superiority is in his attainments, practices and principles, which if they are not always moral, are above meanness, and he has usually no pride in the mere vulgar consequence of wealth. Should he happen to be well born, (for birth is by no means indispensable to the character,) his satisfaction is in being allied to men of the same qualities as himself, and not to a senseless pride in an accident. The vulgar-minded mistake motives that they cannot feel; but he, at least, is capable of distinguishing between things that are false, and the things which make him what he is.

An eminent writer of our own time, has said in substance, that a nation is happy, in which the people, possessing the power to select their rulers, select the noble. This was the opinion of a European, who had been accustomed to see the liberal qualities in the exclusive possession of a caste, and who was not accustomed to see the people sufficiently advanced to mingle in affairs of state. Power cannot be extended to a *caste*, without *caste's* reaping its principle benefit; but happy, indeed, is the nation, in which, power being the common property, there is sufficient discrimination and justice to admit the intelligent and refined to a just participation of its influence.

An Aristocrat and a Democrat

WE live in an age, when the words aristocrat and democrat are much used, without regard to the real significations. An aristocrat is one of a few, who possess the political power of a country; a democrat, one of the many. The words are also properly applied to those who entertain notions favorable to aristocratical, or democratical forms of government. Such persons are not, necessarily, either aristocrats, or democrats in fact, but merely so in opinion. Thus a member of a democratical government may have an aristocratical bias, and *vice versa*.

To call a man who has the habits and opinions of a gentleman, an aristocrat, from that fact alone, is an abuse of terms, and betrays ignorance of the true principles of government, as well as of the world. It must be an equivocal freedom, under which every one is not the master of his own innocent acts and associations, and he is a sneaking democrat, indeed, who will submit to be dictated to, in those habits over which neither law nor morality assumes a right of control.

Some men fancy that a democrat can only be one who seeks the level, social, mental and moral, of the majority, a rule that would at once exclude all men of refinement, education and taste from the class. These persons are enemies of democracy, as they at once render it impracticable. They are usually great sticklers for their own associations and habits, too, though unable to comprehend any of a nature that are superior. They are, in truth, aristocrats in principle, though assuming a contrary pretension; the ground work of all their feelings and arguments being self. Such is not the intention of liberty, whose aim is to leave every man to be the master of his own acts; denying hereditary honors, it is true, as unjust and unnecessary, but not denying the inevitable consequences of civilization.

The law of God is the only rule of conduct, in this, as in other matters. Each man should do as he would be done by. Were the question put to the greatest advocate of indiscriminate association, whether he would submit to have his company and habits dictated to him, he would be one of the first to resist the tyranny; for they, who are the most rigid in maintaining their own claims, in such matters, are usually the loudest in decrying those whom they fancy to be better off than themselves. Indeed, it may be taken as a rule in social intercourse, that he who is the most apt to question the pretensions of others, is the most conscious of the doubtful position he himself occupies; thus establishing the very claims he affects to deny, by letting his jealousy of it be seen. Manners, education and refinement, are positive things, and they bring with them innocent tastes which are productive of high enjoyments; and it is as unjust to deny their possessors their indulgence, as it would be to insist on the less fortunate's passing the time they would rather devote to athletic amusements, in listening to operas for which they have no relish, sung in a language they do not understand.

All that democracy means, is as equal a participation in rights as is practicable; and to pretend that social equality is a condition of popular institutions, is to assume that the latter are destructive of civilization, for, as nothing is more self-evident than the impossibility of raising all men to the highest standard of tastes and refinement, the alternative would be to reduce the entire community to the lowest. The whole embarrassment on this point exists in the difficulty of making men comprehend qualities they do not themselves possess. We can all perceive the difference between ourselves and our inferiors, but when it comes to a question of the difference between us and our superiors, we fail to appreciate merits of which we have no proper conceptions. In face of this obvious difficulty, there is the safe and just governing rule, already mentioned, or that of permitting every one to be the undisturbed judge of his own habits and associations, so long as they are innocent, and do not impair the rights of others to be equally judges for themselves. It follows, that social intercourse must regulate itself, independently of institutions, with the exception that the latter, while they withold no natural, bestow no factitious advantages beyond those which are inseparable from the rights of property, and general civilization.

In a democracy, men are just as free to aim at the highest attainable places in society, as to obtain the largest fortunes; and it would be clearly unworthy of all noble sentiment to say, that the grovelling competition for money shall alone be free, while that which enlists all the liberal acquirements and elevated sentiments of the race, is denied the democrat. Such an avowal would be at once, a declaration of the inferiority of the system, since nothing but ignorance and vulgarity could be its fruits.

The democratic gentleman must differ in many essential particulars, from the aristocratical gentleman, though in their ordinary habits and tastes they are virtually indentical. Their principles vary; and, to a slight degree, their deportment accordingly. The democrat, recognizing the right of all to participate in power, will be more liberal in his general sentiments, a quality of superiority in itself; but, in conceding this much to his fellow man, he will proudly maintain his own independence of vulgar domination, as indispensable to his personal habits. The same principles and manliness that would induce him to depose a royal despot, would induce him to resist a vulgar tyrant.

There is no more capital, though more common error, than to suppose him an aristocrat who maintains his independence of habits; for democracy asserts the control of the majority, only, in matters of law, and not in matters of custom. The very object of the institution is the utmost practicable personal liberty, and to affirm the contrary, would be sacrificing the end to the means.

An aristocrat, therefore, is merely one who fortifies his exclusive privileges by positive institutions, and a democrat, one who is willing to admit of a free competition, in all things. To say, however, that the last supposes this competition will lead to nothing, is an assumption that means are employed without any reference to an end. He is the purest democrat who best maintains his rights, and no rights can be dearer to a man of cultivation, than exemptions from unseasonable invasions on his time, by the coarse-minded and ignorant.

On Demagogues

A DEMAGOGUE, in the strict signification of the word, is 'a leader of the rabble.' It is a Greek compound, that conveys this meaning. In these later times, however, the signification has been extended to suit the circumstances of the age. Thus, before the art of printing became known, or cheap publications were placed within the reach of the majority, the mass of all nations might properly enough be termed a rabble, when assembled in bodies. In nations in which attention is paid to education, this reproach is gradually becoming unjust, though a body of Americans, even, collected under what is popularly termed an 'excitement,' losing sight of that reason and respect for their own deliberately framed ordinances, which alone distinguish them from the masses of other people, is neither more nor less than a rabble. Men properly derive their designations from their acts, and not from their professions.

The peculiar office of a demogogue is to advance his own interests, by affecting a deep devotion to the interests of the people. Sometimes the object is to indulge malignancy, unprincipled and selfish men submitting but to two governing motives, that of doing good to themselves, and that of doing harm to others. The true theatre of a demagogue is a democracy, for the body of the community possessing the power, the master he pretends to serve is best able to reward his efforts. As it is all important to distinguish between those who labor in behalf of the people on the general account, and those who labor in behalf of the people on their own account, some of the rules by which each may be known shall be pointed out.

The motive of the demagogue may usually be detected in his conduct. The man who is constantly telling the people that they are unerring in judgment, and that they have all power, is a demagogue. Bodies of men being composed of individuals, can no more be raised above the commission of error, than individuals themselves, and, in many situations, they are more likely to err, from self-excitement and the division of responsibility. The power of the people is limited by the fundamental laws, or the constitution, the rights and opinions of the minority, in all but those cases in which a decision becomes indispensable, being just as sacred as the rights and opinions of the majority; else would a democracy be, indeed, what its enemies term it, the worst species of tyranny. In this instance, the people are flattered, in order to be led; as in kingdoms, the prince is blinded to his own defects, in order to extract favor from him.

The demagogue always puts the people before the constitution and the laws, in face of the obvious truth that the people have placed the constitution and the laws before themselves.

The local demagogue does not distinguish between the whole people and a part of the people, and is apt to betray his want of principles by contending for fancied, or assumed rights, in favor of a county, or a town, though the act is obviously opposed to the will of the nation. This is a test that the most often betrays the demagogue, for while loudest in proclaiming his devotion to the majority, he is, in truth, opposing the will of the entire people, in order to effect his purposes with a part.

The demagogue is usually sly, a detractor of others, a professor of humility and disinterestedness, a great stickler for equality as respects all above him, a man who acts in corners, and avoids open and manly expositions of his course, calls blackguards gentlemen, and gentlemen folks, appeals to passions and prejudices rather than to reason, and is in all respects, a man of intrigue and deception, of sly cunning and management, instead of manifesting the frank, fearless qualities of the democracy he so prodigally professes.

The man who maintains the rights of the people on pure grounds, may be distinguished from the demagogue by the reverse of all these qualities. He does not flatter the people, even while he defends them, for he knows that flattery is a corrupting and dangerous poison. Having nothing to conceal, he is frank and fearless, as are all men with the consciousness of right motives. He oftener chides than commends, for power needs reproof and can dispense with praise.

He who would be a courtier under a king, is almost certain to be a demagogue in a democracy. The elements are the same, though, brought into action under different circumstances, ordinary observers are apt to fancy them the extremes of opposite moral castes. Travellers have often remarked, that, Americans, who have made themselves conspicuous abroad for their adulation of rank and power, have become zealous advocates of popular supremacy, on returning home. Several men of this stamp are, at this moment, in conspicuous political stations in the country, having succeeded by the commonest arts of courtiers.

There is a large class of political men in this country, who, while they scarcely merit the opprobrium of being termed demagogues, are not properly exempt from the imputation of falling into some of their most dangerous vices. These are they, whose habits, and tastes, and better opinions, indeed, are all at variance with vulgar errors and vulgar practices, but, who imagine it a necessary evil in a democracy to defer to prejudices, and ignorance, and even to popular jealousies and popular injustice, that a safe direction may be given to the publick mind. Such men deceive themselves, in the first place, as to their own motives, which are rather their private advancement than the publick good, and, admitting the motives to be pure, they err greatly both in their mode of construing the system under which they live, and in the general principles of correcting evil and of producing good. As the greatest enemy of truth is falsehood, so is the most potent master of falsehood, truth. These qualities are correlatives; that which is not true, being false; and that which is not false, being true. It follows, as a pervading rule of morals, that the advancement of one is the surest means of defeating the other. All good men desire the truth, and, on all publick occasions on which it is necessary to act at all, the truth would be the most certain, efficient, and durable agency in defeating falsehoods, whether of prejudices, reports, or principles. The perception of truth is an attribute of reason, and the ground-work of all institutions that claim to be founded in justice, is this high quality. Temporary convenience, and selfish considerations, beyond a doubt, are both favored by sometimes closing the eyes to the severity of truth, but in nothing is the sublime admonition of God in his commandments, where he tells us that he 'will visit the sins of the fathers unto the third and fourth generations of their children,' more impressively verified, than in the inevitable punishments that await every sacrifice of truth.

Most of the political men of the day belong to this class of doubtful moralists, who, mistaking a healthful rule, which admonishes us that even truth ought not to be too offensively urged, in their desire to be moderate, lend themselves to the side of error. The ingenuity of sophisms, and the audacity of falsehoods receive great support from this mistaken alliance, since a firm union of all the intelligent of a country, in the cause of plain and obvious truths, would exterminate their correlative errors, the publick opinion which is now enlisted in the support of the latter, following to the right side, as a matter of course, in the train of combined knowledge. This is the mode in which opinions rooted in the wrong have been gradually eradicated, by the process of time, but which would yield faster, were it not for the latitude and delusion that selfishness imposes on men of this class, who flatter themselves with soothing a sore that they are actually irritating. The consequence of this mistaken forbearance, is to substitute a new set of errors, for those which it has already taken ages to get rid of.

On the subject of government and society, it is a misfortune that this country is filled with those who take the opposite extremes, the one side clinging to prejudices that were founded in the abuses of the feudal times, and the other to the exaggerations of impracticable theories. That the struggle is not fiercer, is probably owing to the overwhelming numbers of the latter class, but, as things are, truth is a sufferer.

The American *doctrinaire* is the converse of the American demagogue, and, in his way, is scarcely less injurious to the publick. He is as much a visionary on one side, as the extreme theoretical democrat is a visionary on the other. The first deals in poetry, the last in cant. The first affirms a disinterestedness and purity in education and manners, when exposed to the corruption of power, that all experience refutes; and the last an infallibility in majorities that God himself has denied. These opposing classes produce the effect of all counter-acting forces, resistance, and they provoke each other's excesses.

In the *doctrinaire*, or theorist of the old school, we see men clinging to opinions that are purely the issue of arbitrary facts, ages after the facts themselves have ceased to exist, confounding cause with effect; and, in the demagogue, or his tool, the impracticable democrat, one who permits envy, jealousy, opposition, selfishness, and the unconsciousness of his own inferiority and demerits, so far to blind his faculties, as to obscure the sense of justice, to exclude the sight of positive things, and to cause him to deny the legitimate consequences of the very laws of which he professes to be proud. This is the dupe who affirms that, 'one man is as good as another.'

These extremes lead to the usual inconsistencies and follies. Thus do we see men, who sigh for titles and factitious and false distinctions, so little conscious of truth, as to shrink from asserting the real distinctions of their social station, or those they actually and undeniably possess; as if nature ever intended a man for an aristocrat, who has not the manhood to maintain his just rights; and those, again, who cant of equality and general privileges, while they stubbornly refuse to permit others to enjoy in peace a single fancied indulgence or taste, unless taken in their company, although nature, education and habits have all unfitted them to participate, and their presence would be sure to defeat what they could not, in the nature of things, enjoy.

The considerate, and modest, and just-minded man, of whatever social class, will view all this differently. In asserting his own rights, he respects those of others; in indulging his own tastes, he is willing to admit there may be superior; in pursuing his own course, in his own manner, he knows his neighbor has an equal right to do the same; and, most of all, is he impressed with the great moral truths, that flatterers are inherently miscreants, that fallacies never fail to bring their punishments, and that the empire of God is reason.

On Representation

REPRESENTATION is the vital principle of all free governments, with the exception of those which rule over unusually small territories. A pure democracy infers institutions under which the people, in primary assemblies, enact their own laws; a system of which the good is questionable under any circumstances, and which is evidently impracticable in large communities. The governments of the several states of this Union, with some slight modifications, are representative democracies, and as the federal government receives its distinctive character from the states, themselves, the latter is necessarily a confederated representative democracy. Representation, therefore, lies at the root of the entire American system.

Conflicting opinions exist on the subject of the relations between the representative and his constituent, impracticable notions and contradictory errors being equally maintained. These notions may be divided into those of two schools, equally ultra, one taking its rise in the sophisms and mystifications of English politics, the other arising from the disposition of men to obtain their objects, by flattering popular power. The subject is grave, and all important to a country like this.

With the exception of a few popular boroughs, and a county or two, England has no free representation. In most of the counties, even, the control of the elections is in the hands of the great land-holders; in far the larger number of the boroughs, the power of the landlords is so great, that they name the successful candidate, as openly as the minister himself names to official employments. In the case of contested elections, even, the struggle is really between the power of two or more great families, and not between bodies of the electors, seats for boroughs being bought and sold like any other commodity. Under such circumstances, it is quite apparent that instructions from a constituency, that is itself instructed whom to return, would be a useless mockery. We are not to look at England, therefore, for principles on this subject, the fundamental systems of the two countries being so dissimilar; one giving power to property, the other to numbers.

There is no doubt it is the intention of the American system, that the will of the constitutional majorities, to a certain extent, should be properly regarded by the representative; and that when the latter, who has been elected with the express understanding that he is to support a particular measure, or a particular set of principles, sees reason to change his opinion, he would act most in conformity with the spirit of the institutions, by resigning his trust. All human contracts are made subject to certain predominant moral obligations, which are supposed to emanate from Divine Truth. Thus, a representative, conscientiously entertaining convictions in its favour, may give a pledge to support a particular measure, as a condition of his election, there being no sufficient reason to doubt that the doctrine of specific pledges is sound, the people having a free option to exact them, and the candidate as free an option to withhold them, as each may see fit. These pledges, however, must be in conformity with the spirit and letter of the constitution, and not opposed to good morals; the first being a governing condition of the social compact, and the last a controlling principle of human actions. But, while this much is admitted in favor of the power of the constituency, great care must be had not to extend it too far.

In the first place, no constituency has a right to violate the honest convictions of a representative. These are a matter of conscience, and, if the subject be of sufficient magnitude to involve conscientious scruples, the power of the representative is full and absolute. This freedom of conscience is an implied obligation of the compact between the parties; therefore, in a case of importance, that admits of moral doubts, and one in which the will of the constituency is unequivocally expressed, it becomes the representative to return the trust, and this, too, in season, circumstances allowing, to permit the other party to be represented in the matter, agreeably to its own opinions. As there are so many governing circumstances of great delicacy, in all such cases, it is evident they must be rare, and that the rule exists as an exception, rather than as one of familiar practice.

Great care must be always taken to see that the wishes of

the constituency are actually consulted, before the American representative is bound, morally even, to respect their will; for there is no pretence that the obligation to regard the wishes of his constituents is more than implied, under any circumstances; the social compact, in a legal sense, leaving him the entire master of his own just convictions. The instant a citizen is elected he becomes the representative of the minority as well as of the majority, and to create any of the implied responsibility that has been named, the opinion of the first, so far as their numbers go, is just as much entitled to respect as the opinion of the last. The power to decide, in cases of elections, is given to the majority only from necessity, and as the safest practicable general rule that can be used, but, it is by no means the intention of the institutions to disfranchise all those who prefer another to the successful candidate. The choice depends on a hundred considerations that are quite independent of measures, men judging differently from each other, in matters of character. Any other rule than this might be made the means of putting the government in the hands of the minority, as the following case will show.

A, is elected to congress, by a vote of one thousand and one, against a vote of nine hundred and ninety-nine. He has, consequently, two thousand constituents, supposing all to have voted. The majority meet to instruct their representative, and the instructions are carried by a vote of five hundred and one to five hundred. If these instructions are to be received as binding, the government, so far as the particular measure is concerned, may be in the hands of five hundred and one electors, as opposed to fourteen hundred and ninety-nine. This case may be modified, by all the changes incidental to numbers.

To assume that majorities of caucuses, or of *ex parte* collections of electors, have a right to instruct, is to pretend that the government is a government of party, and not a government of the people. This notion cannot honestly be maintained for an instant. Recommendations emanating from such a source may be entitled to a respectful consideration, but not more so than a counter-recommendation from an opposing party. In all such cases, the intention of the representative system is to constitute the representative a judge between the conflicting opinions, as judges at law are intended to settle questions of law, both being sworn to act on the recognized principles that control society.

In the cases that plainly invade the constitution, the constituents having no power themselves, can dictate none to their representative. Both parties are bound equally to respect that instrument, and neither can evade the obligation, by any direct, or indirect means. This rule covers much of the disputed ground, for they who read the constitution with an honest desire to understand it, can have little difficulty in comprehending most of its important provisions, and no one can claim a right to impose sophistry and selfishness on another, as reason and justice.

As doubtful cases may certainly arise under the constitution, the right of the constituency to influence the representative in instances of that sort, may plausibly be supposed to be greater than in those of constructions plainly proceeding from the excitement and schemes of partisans. Still the power of the constituency to interfere, *after an election*, beyond the right to urge their own sentiments, as opinions entitled to particular respect from their particular representative, is very questionable. The constitution contains the paramount laws of society. These laws are unchangeable, except as they are altered agreeably to prescribed forms, and until thus altered, no evasion of them is admissible. In the necessity of things, every public functionary must be permitted to interpret this instrument for himself, subject to the liabilities and responsibilities, official and otherwise, of his station. In this respect, the legislator, by the nature of his trust, having full power to enact and to repeal, knows no other control than his conscience. The expressed com-

pact between the representative and the constituent, gives
to the first an absolute discretionary power, subject to this
great rule, and, by the implied, no instructions can ever
weaken this high obligation since it is clearly a governing
condition of the bargain between them.

A judge is representative, in a government like this, in a
general sense, since he acts for and through the people.
Now, it will not be pretended that the people can instruct
the courts how to interpret the constitution, although they
can alter it, nor should it be contended that the constituency
can instruct a representative how to interpret the constitution, when it involves a matter of conscience. The remedy,
in the one case, is to alter the constitution; and in the other,
to send a new representative, with pledges given previously
to the election, to interpret the constitution according to the
conceptions of the right, entertained by the constituency. Of
course such a pledge ought not to be given, unless given
conscientiously.

The constitution specifically guaranties the right of the
citizens to assemble and *petition* congress, a provision that
would be a mockery, did that instrument suppose a right
to *instruct*.

It has been said that the representative, has the same
relations to the minority, as to the majority of his constituents, when elected. In a broader and equally binding sense,
he has the same relations to the entire country, as to his
own immediate constituents, else would legislation be reduced to a mere contest of local interests, without a regard
to justice or to general principles. If this be true, and it must
be true, or all the fundamental governing rules of the social
compact become of no account, the constituents of a particular representative can have no right even to request,
much less to instruct him to support their local interests at
the expence of others, and least of all they can have a right
to violate the constitution, in order to do so. In this particular, the question has been involved in the same sophisms,

as those which appertain to the relations between the accused and his legal counsel. Some latitudinarians in morals have contended that the legal adviser of an accused has a right to do in his defence, whatever the accused himself would do; that he is an attorney, with full powers to execute all that the other's feelings, interests and passions might dictate. This is monstrous and untenable doctrine, being destructive of all moral responsibility, to say nothing of the laws. The counsel, has a *right* to do no more than his client has a *right* to do, nor can the constituent, in any case, have a right to instruct his representative to do that which he has no right, in a moral or legal sense to do himself, even admitting the general doctrine of instruction to be sound.

Although the principle that the representative chosen by a few, becomes the representative of all, is sound as a general principle, it is not an unqualified rule any where, and still less so in the federal government. The constitution requires that the representative should reside in the state from which he is sent, expressly to identify him with its particular interests, and in order to prevent that concentration which exists in other countries. Half the French deputies are from Paris, and a large portion of the English members of parliament are virtually from the capital. Their systems are peculiarly systems of concentration, but ours is as peculiarly a system of diffusion. It may be questioned, therefore, how far the American representative ought to sacrifice the good of his particular state, in order to achieve the general good. Cases may certainly occur, in which the sacrifice ought to be made, but the union of these states is founded on an express compromise, and it is not its intention to reach a benefit, however considerable, by extorting undue sacrifices from particular members of the confederacy. All cases to the contrary should be clear, and the necessary relations between the good and evil, beyond cavil.

In identified governments, the principle that a few shall be sacrificed to the general good, must always, in a greater or less degree, prevail; but it is not the intention of the American compact that any one state should ruin itself, or even do itself any great and irreparable injury, that the rest of the Union should become more prosperous. In this sense, then, the member of congress represents his immediate constituents, or perhaps it would be better to say his immediate state, and although he has no right to further its interests at the expense of the interests of other states, he is not called on to sacrifice them for the benefit of the sisters of the Union. This is one of the cases in which the doctrines of English representation do not apply to the American system. The difference arises from the circumstance that, in the one case, government is a compact between persons; in the other, a compact between states.

In a government like that of the United States, the executive is as much representative as the legislature. Will it therefore be pretended that the president is also bound to respect the instructions of the people? Is he to appoint those whom the people will, remove those whom the people denounce, pardon those whom the people order, and approve of such bills as the people dictate? Is he to command the army and navy, see that the laws are executed, and conduct the negotiations of the country according to the opinions and intimations of a majority of his constituents, or according to his own conceptions of duty, and the light of his own knowledge and experience? If the representative is bound to obey the will of his constituents, all this must the president do, or prove false to the institutions. As the commander in chief, his own soldiers would have a right to instruct him in the mode of performing his military functions, as, indeed, they would have a right to tell congress, when and against whom to declare war!

If the representative of the executive functions is thus bound to respect instructions, a majority of the people might virtually repeal an unpopular law, by instructing the president not to see it enforced, and thus destroy the rights of third parties. Such a doctrine would throw society into confusion, leave nothing stable, and set up a dangerous and irresponsible power, that would be stronger than the institutions themselves.

A principle reason for sending representatives to congress, is the impossibility of masses of men meeting to legislate with due knowledge and deliberation, and it can scarcely be contended that the results which cannot be obtained by any expedient of law, method and arrangement, are to be expected from extra-legal, voluntary and immethodical means. We ought not, consequently, to give an authority to those opinions of the people informally expressed, that the constitution would seem to show cannot be rendered available, when formally expressed.

The term representative implies full power to act, or, at least, full power to act under the limitations that environ the trust. A delegate is less gifted with authority, and is understood to act under instructions. These are ancient distinctions, and, existing as they did at the time the constitution was framed, they are entitled to respect, as explaining its intention. A representative is a *substitute*; a delegate an *ambassador*. It is, moreover, an admission of imbecility to suppose that the institutions infer a right to instruct, when no such right is expressed. All the machinery of the state is opposed to it, while in other countries, as in Switzerland, where the delegate acts under instructions, the machinery of the state is framed to meet such an end.

Upon the whole, when we take into consideration the received signification of terms, as they were understood when the constitution was framed; the legal effect of legislative acts, which are binding, though the entire constituency instruct to the contrary; the omission in the constitution to point out any legal means of instructing, and the practical difficulties in obtaining instructions that shall be above the reproach of being *ex parte* and insufficient; the permanent obligations of the constitution; the doubt and indecision instructions would introduce into a government, that was expressly framed to obviate these weaknesses; the dangers that constantly arise from the activity of the designing, and the supineness of the well-meaning; the want of unity, and of fixed principles, it might give to a legislation that controls peace and war, and the foreign relations; as well as the exposure to foreign influence directly exercised over irresponsible men; and the general character of deliberation and examination which is secured to congress, which may be called on to act on information known only to itself; we are led to conclude that the doctrine of instruction is unconstitutional, whether as applied to the senate, or to the house of representatives, and that so far from being a doctrine that is adapted to secure the domination of real majorities, it is rather an invention of intriguing politicians to effect their own wishes, in opposition to those of the nation. Exceptions may occur, but governing principles are to be settled on general rules, and by general effects.

It being established that the representative is placed beyond the control of instructions, as beyond doubt is, at least, his legal position, the importance of making careful selections, becomes apparent. There is no safer rule in selecting a representative, than that already named; or that of choosing the man for public confidence, who may be relied on, in private. Most of all is the time-server and demagogue to be avoided, for such a man is certain to use power as an instrument of his private good. It is a mistake to suppose, on correct principles, that the representative is the obliged party. The man who faithfully does his duty in congress, is a servant to whom a difficult task is assigned, with a very insufficient compensation; and such a man should always be selected with care, and rewarded with a frank gratitude.

It is a painful admission, extorted by truth, that in human institutions, the intention is never long respected. Representation may not be in practice, what it was intended for, in theory, but, still, it might be drawn much nearer to what it ought to be, than it actually is. If party be not necessary to this government as a good, it is, perhaps, unavoidable as an evil. But no elector should ever submit himself so implicitly to party as to support a man whose private acts prove him to be unfit for a public trust. The basis of the representative system is character, and without character, no man should be confided in. In discriminating between candidates, however, it should be remembered that there are 'wolves in sheep's clothing,' in character, as well as in other things. Personal vanity induces ordinary men to confide most in those who most flatter their frailties, but, it is a tolerably safe rule that he who is not afraid to speak the truth, is not afraid to act the truth; and truths, moral, political and social, are peculiarly the aim of this government.

On Candor

CANDOR is a proof of both a just frame of mind, and of a good tone of breeding. It is a quality that belongs, equally to the honest man and to the gentleman: to the first, as doing to others as we would ourselves be done by; to the last, as indispensable to the liberality of the character.

By candor we are not to understand trifling and uncalled for expositions of truth; but a sentiment that proves a conviction of the necessity of speaking truth, when speaking at all; a contempt for all designing evasions of our real opinions; and a deep conviction that he who deceives by necessary implication, deceives wilfully.

In all the general concerns, the publick has a right to be treated with candor. Without this manly and truly republican quality, republican because no power exists in the country to intimidate any from its exhibition, the institutions are converted into a stupendous fraud.

Foreigners reproach the Americans with a want of direct-
ness and candor, in conducting their ordinary intercourse.
It is said that they dissemble thoughts that might properly
be expressed, in the presence of the parties interested, to
express them openly and in a way to insinuate more than is
asserted, behind their backs. It is to be feared that this is
a vice of humanity, but, still, one people may be more under
its influence than another. It would be a singular and a
false effect of freedom, to destroy a nation's character for
candor; but we are not to be deceived by names, it being
quite possible that a tyranny of opinion should produce
such results, even in a democracy.

America is under many powerful influences, that have
little connection with the institutions. The want of large
towns, the scattered population, and the absence of much
marked inequality of condition, necessarily lend a provincial
character to the population, a character that every where
favors the natural propensity of man to bring all his fellows
within the control of his own strictures. The religionists
who first settled the country, too, have aided in bringing
individual opinion in subjection to publick opinion, and, as
the latter is always controlled by combinations and design,
consequently more or less to error. There is no doubt that
these combined causes have had the effect to make a large
portion of the population less direct, frank, candid and
simple in the expression of their honest sentiments, and
even in the relation of facts, than the laws of God, and the
social duties require. It is to this feeling that the habit has
arisen of making cautious and evasive answers, such as 'I
guess,' 'I conclude,' 'I some think,' 'I shouldn't wonder, if
such a man had said so and so,' when the speaker is the
whole time confident of the fact. This practice has the reproach of insincerity and equivocation, is discreditable,
makes intercourse treacherous and unsafe, and is beneath
the frankness of freemen. In all these respects, a majority
of the American people might take a useful lesson from

the habits of England, a country which though remarkable for servility to superiors, can boast of more frankness in ordinary life, than our own.

Candor has the high merit of preventing misconceptions, simplifies intercourse, prevents more misunderstandings than equivocation, elevates character, inculcates the habit of sincerity, and has a general tendency to the manly and virtuous qualities.

On Language

LANGUAGE being the medium of thought, its use enters into our most familiar practices. A just, clear and simple expression of our ideas is a necessary accomplishment for all who aspire to be classed with gentlemen and ladies. It renders all more respectable, besides making intercourse more intelligible, safer and more agreeable.

The common faults of American language are an ambition to effect, a want of simplicity, and a turgid abuse of terms. To these may be added ambiguity of expression. Many perversions of significations also exist, and a formality of speech, which, while it renders conversation ungraceful, and destroys its playfulness, seriously weakens the power of the language, by applying to ordinary ideas, words that are suited only to themes of gravity and dignity.

While it is true that the great body of the American people use their language more correctly than the mass of any other considerable nation, it is equally true that a smaller proportion than common attain to elegance in this accomplishment, especially in speech. Contrary to the general law in such matters, the women of the country have a less agreeable utterance than the men, a defect that great care should be taken to remedy, as the nursery is the birthplace of so many of our habits.

The limits of this work will not permit an enumeration of the popular abuses of significations, but a few shall be mentioned, in order that the student may possess a general clue to the faults. 'Creek,' a word that signifies an *inlet* of the sea, or of a lake, is misapplied to running streams, and frequently to the *outlets* of lakes. A 'square,' is called a 'park;' 'lakes,' are often called 'ponds;' and 'arms of the sea,' are sometimes termed 'rivers.'

In pronunciation, the faults are still more numerous, partaking decidedly of provincialisms. The letter *u*, sounded like a double *o*, or *oo*, or like *i*, as in vir*too*, for*tin*, for*tinate*; and *ew*, pronounced also like *oo*, are common errors. This is an exceedingly vicious pronunciation, rendering the language mean and vulgar. 'New,' pronounced as '*noo*,' is an example, and 'few,' as '*foo*;' the true sounds are '*nu*' and '*fu*,' the *u* retaining its proper soft sound, and not that of '*oo*.'

The attempt to reduce the pronunciation of the English language to a common rule, produces much confusion, and taking the usages of polite life as the standard, many uncouth innovations. All know the pronounciation of plough; but it will scarcely do to take this sound as the only power of the same combination of final letters, for we should be compelled to call though, thou; through, throu; and tough, tou.

False accentuation is a common American fault. Ensign (insin,) is called en*syne*, and engine (injin,) en*gyne*. Indeed, it is a common fault of narrow associations, to suppose that words are to be pronounced as they are spelled.

Many words are in a state of mutation, the pronunciation being unsettled even in the best society, a result that must often arise where language is as variable and undetermined as the English. To this class belong 'clerk,' and 'cucumber' and 'gold,' which are often pronounced as spelt, though it were better and more in conformity with polite usage to say 'clark,' '*cow*-cumber,' (not cow*cumber*,) and 'goold.' For *looten*ant (lieutenant) there is not sufficient authority, the true pronunciation being '*levten*ant.' By making a familiar compound of this word, we see the uselesness of attempting to reduce the language to any other laws than those of the usages of polite life, for they who affect to say *looten*ant, do not say '*looten*ant-co-lo-nel,' but '*looten*ant-kurnel.'

The polite pronunciation of 'either' and 'neither' is 'i-ther' and 'ni-ther,' and not 'eether' and 'neether.' This is a case in which the better usage of the language has respected derivations, for '*ei*,' in German are pronounced as in 'height' and 'sleight,' '*ie*' making the sound of '*ee*.' We see the arbitrary usages of the English, however, by comparing these legitimate sounds with those of the words 'lieutenant colonel,' which are derived from the French, in which language the latter word is called '*co-lo-nel*.'

Some changes of the language are to be regretted, as they lead to false inferences, and society is always a loser by mistaking names for things. Life is a fact, and it is seldom any good arises from a misapprehension of the real circumstances under which we exist. The word 'gentleman' has a positive and limited signification. It means one elevated above the mass of society by his birth, manners, attainments, character and social condition. As no civilized society can exist without these social differences, nothing is gained by denying the use of the term. If blackguards were to be *called* 'gentlemen,' and 'gentlemen,' 'blackguards,' the difference between them would be as obvious as it is to-day.

The word 'gentleman,' is derived from the French gentil-homme, which originally signified one of noble birth. This was at a time when the characteristics of the condition were never found beyond a caste. As society advanced, ordinary men attained the qualifications of nobility, without that of birth, and the meaning of the word was extended. It is now possible to be a gentleman without birth, though, even in America, where such distinctions are purely conditional, they who have birth, except in extraordinary instances, are classed with gentlemen. To call a laborer, one who has neither education, manners, accomplishments, tastes, associations, nor any one of the ordinary requisites, a gentleman, is just as absurd as to call one who is thus qualified, a fellow. The word must have some especial signification, or it would be synonymous with man. One may have gentleman-like feelings, principles and appearance, without possessing the liberal attainments that distinguish the ciations, nor any one of the ordinary requisites, a gentleman, though, as it becomes a means of obtaining the other requisites, it is usual to give it a place in the claims of the class. Men may be, and often are, very rich without having the smallest title to be deemed gentlemen. A man may be a distinguished gentleman, and not possess as much money as his own footman.

This word, however, is sometimes used instead of the old terms, 'sirs,' 'my masters,' &c. &c., as in addressing bodies of men. Thus we say 'gentlemen,' in addressing a publick meeting, in complaisance, and as, by possibility, some gentlemen may be present. This is a license that may be tolerated, though he who should insist that all present were, as individuals, gentlemen, would hardly escape ridicule.

What has just been said of the word gentleman, is equally true with that of lady. The standard of these two classes, rises as society becomes more civilized and refined; the man who might pass for a gentleman in one nation, or community, not being able to maintain the same position in another.

The inefficiency of the effort to subvert things by names, is shown in the fact that, in all civilized communities, there is a class of men, who silently and quietly recognize each other, as gentlemen; who associate together freely and without reserve, and who admit each other's claims without scruple or distrust. This class may be limited by prejudice and arbitrary enactments, as in Europe, or it may have no other rules than those of taste, sentiment and the silent laws of usage, as in America.

The same observations may be made in relation to the words master and servant. He who employs laborers, with the right to command, is a master, and he who lets himself to work with an obligation to obey, a servant. Thus there are house, or domestic servants, farm servants, shop servants, and various other servants; the term master being in all these cases the correlative.

In consequence of the domestic servants of America having once been negro-slaves, a prejudice has arisen among the laboring classes of the whites, who not only dislike the term servant, but have also rejected that of master. So far has this prejudice gone, that in lieu of the latter, they have resorted to the use of the word *boss*, which has precisely the same meaning in Dutch! How far a subterfuge of this nature is worthy of a manly and common sense people, will admit of question.

A similar objection may be made to the use of the word 'help,' which is not only an innovation on a just and established term, but which does not properly convey the meaning intended. They who aid their master in the toil may be deemed 'helps,' but they who perform all the labor do not assist, or help to do the thing, but they do it themselves. A man does not usually hire his cook to *help* him cook his dinner, but to cook it herself. Nothing is therefore gained, while something is lost in simplicity and clearness by the substitution of new and imperfect terms, for the long established words of language. In all cases in which the people of America have retained the *things* of their ancestors, they should not be ashamed to keep the *names*.

The love of turgid expressions is gaining ground, and ought to be corrected. One of the most certain evidences of a man of high breeding, is his simplicity of speech; a simplicity that is equally removed from vulgarity and exaggeration. He calls a spade, a 'spade.' His enunciation, while clear, deliberate and dignified, is totally without strut, showing his familiarity with the world, and, in some degree, reflecting the qualities of his mind, which is polished without being addicted to sentimentalism, or any other bloated feeling. He never calls his wife, 'his lady,' but 'his wife,' and he is not afraid of lessening the dignity of the human race, by styling the most elevated and refined of his fellow creatures, 'men and women.' He does not say, in speaking of a dance, that 'the attire of the ladies was exceedingly elegant and peculiarly becoming at the late assembly,' but that 'the women were well dressed at the last ball;' nor is he apt to remark, 'that the Rev. Mr G— gave us an elegant and searching discourse the past sabbath,' but that 'the parson preached a good sermon last sunday.'

The utterance of a gentleman ought to be deliberate and clear, without being measured. All idea of effort should be banished, though nothing lost for want of distinctness. His emphasis ought to be almost imperceptible; never halting, or abrupt; and least of all, so placed as to give an idea of his own sense of cleverness; but regulated by those slight intonations that give point to wit, and force to reason. His language should rise with the subject, and, as he must be an educated and accomplished man, he cannot but know that the highest quality of eloquence, and all sublimity, is in the thought, rather than in the words, though there must be an adaptation of the one to the other.

This is still more true of women than of men, since the former are the natural agents in maintaining the refinement of a people.

All cannot reach the highest standard in such matters, for it depends on early habit, and particularly on early associations. The children of gentlemen are as readily distinguished from other children by these peculiarities, as by the greater delicacy of their minds, and higher tact in breeding. But we are not to abandon all improvement, because perfection is reached but by few. Simplicity should be the first aim, after one is removed from vulgarity, and let the finer shades of accomplishment be acquired as they can be attained. In no case, however, can one who aims at turgid language, exaggerated sentiments, or pedantic utterance, lay claim to be either a man or a woman of the world.

On the Press

It would seem that providence, for some of its own great ends, has denied to man any particular blessing, which his own waywardness is not destined to lessen, if not entirely to neutralize. In nothing connected with human happiness, is this grave truth more apparent than in the history of the press.

In despotisms, where the weakness of the bodies of nations, is derived from an ignorance of their force, and from the want of means to act in concert, the press is the lever by which the thrones of tyrants and prejudices are the most easily overturned, and, under such circumstances, men often contend for privileges in its behalf, that become dangerous to the peace of society, when civil and political rights are obtained.

In a popular government, so far from according an entire immunity from penalties to the press, its abuses are those which society is required, by its very safety, to visit with its heaviest punishments. In a democracy, misleading the publick mind, as regards facts, characters, or principles, is corrupting all that is dear to society at its source, opinion being the fountain whence justice, honors, and the laws, equally flow.

It is a misfortune that necessity has induced men to accord greater license to this formidable engine, in order to obtain liberty, than can be borne with less important objects in view; for the press, like fire, is an excellent servant, but a terrible master.

It may be taken as rules, that without the liberty of the press, there can be no popular liberty in a nation, and with its licentiousness, neither publick honesty, justice, nor a proper regard for character. Of the two, perhaps, that people is the happiest which is deprived altogether of a free press, since private honesty, and a healthful tone of the publick mind are not incompatible with narrow institutions, though neither can well exist under the constant corrupting action of a licentious press.

The governing principle connected with this interest, would seem to depend on a general law, which, under abuses, converts the most beneficial moral agents to be the greatest enemies of the race. The press is equally capable of being made the instrument of elevating man to the highest point of which his faculties admit, or depressing him to the lowest.

In struggling for liberty and emancipation from errors and prejudices, men have not always paused to reflect on the influence of the agents they have employed, when those agents, from contending with a powerful enemy, shall have become conquerors, and have begun to look about them for the fruits of victory. The press, so efficient as the opponent of tyrants, may become despotic itself; it may substitute new errors for those it has eradicated, and, like an individual spoiled by success, may generally abuse its advantages.

Many false notions have been introduced into society, in the desire to vindicate the rights of so powerful an agent. Of these, one of the worst is the admission of a claim in the press to interfere, in any manner, with private character. The good of such an interference, is at the best but doubtful, and the oppression, in those cases in which injustice is done, is of the most intolerable and irreparable kind.

It would be a proper and a just, though an insufficient atonement, in cases of established libel, to vest a power in the courts to compel the libeller to publish, for a series of weeks, or months, or even years, his own condemnation in his own columns, that the antidote might accompany the poison; though it is to be feared, that the possession of popular rights is still too recent, to permit the majority of men to entertain correct notions concerning an instrument that, they rightly fancy, has been so serviceable in the conflict they have just escaped.

It ought never to be forgotten, that the press, contending for natural but forbidden rights, is no more like the press when these rights are obtained, than the man struggling with adversity, and chastened by misfortune, is like the man flushed with success and corrupted by prosperity.

The history of the press is every where the same. In its infancy it is timid, distrustful, and dependant on truth for success. As it acquires confidence with force, it propagates just opinions with energy; scattering errors and repelling falsehood, until it prevails; when abuses rush in, confounding principles, truths, and all else that is estimable, until it becomes a serious matter of doubt whether a community derives most good or evil, from the institution.

On the Liberty of the Press

WHAT is called the liberty of the press, is very generally misconceived. In despotic, or narrow governments, persons, styled censors, are appointed to examine the columns of journals, *before the latter are issued*, with power to suppress all offensive or injurious articles. This, of course, is putting the press under the control of government, and the press is not a free press, since it cannot publish what its editors please. By the liberty of the press, we are to understand, only, an exemption from this restraint, or a condition of things which enables the citizen to publish what he please, as he can utter what he may please with his tongue.

All men, in a civilized country, however, are responsible for what they say, or publish. If a man speak slander against another, he is liable to the individual injuried, in damages. If a man publish a libel, he incurs the same liability. Some persons suppose that the press possesses privileges, in this respect, that are not accorded to individuals; but the reverse is the fact, as a man may utter with impunity, that which he cannot publish with impunity. The distinction arises from the greater circulation, and the greater power to injure, of a published libel, than of a spoken slander. The editor of a journal, therefore, does not possess the same immunities as an editor, that he possesses as a private citizen. Without such a distinction the community would possess a set of men in its bosom, who would enjoy a power to tyrannize over it, with impunity, through its means of publicity.

The liberty of the press, in principle, resembles the liberty to bear arms. In the one case, the constitution guaranties a right to publish; in the other, a right to keep a musket; but he who injures his neighbor with his publications may be punished, as he who injures his neighbor with his musket may be punished.

The constitution of the United States does not guaranty even the right to publish, except as against the laws of congress, as has been previously stated; the real liberty of the press depending altogether on the provisions of the several state governments, in common with most of the other liberties and rights of the citizen.

On the American Press

THE newspaper press of this country is distinguished from that of Europe in several essential particulars. While there are more prints, they are generally of a lower character. It follows that in all in which they are useful, their utility is more diffused through society, and in all in which they are hurtful, the injury they inflict is more wide-spread and corrupting.

The great number of newspapers in America, is a cause of there being so little capital, and consequently so little intelligence, employed in their management. It is also a reason of the inexactitude of much of the news they circulate. It requires a larger investment of capital than is usual in this country, to obtain correct information; while, on the other hand, the great competition renders editors reckless and impatient to fill their columns. To these circumstances may be added the greater influence of vague and unfounded rumours in a vast and thinly settled country, than on a compact population, covering a small surface.

Discreet and observing men have questioned, whether, after excluding the notices of deaths and marriages, one half of the circumstances that are related in the newspapers of America, as facts, are true in their essential features; and, in cases connected with party politics, it may be questioned if even so large a proportion can be set down as accurate.

This is a terrible picture to contemplate, for when the number of prints is remembered, and the avidity with which they are read is brought into the account, we are made to perceive that the entire nation, in a moral sense, breathes an atmosphere of falsehoods. There is little use, however, in concealing the truth; on the contrary, the dread in which publick men and writers commonly stand of the power of the press to injure them, has permitted the evil to extend so far, that it is scarcely exceeding the bounds of a just alarm, to say that the country cannot much longer exist in safety, under the malign influence that now overshadows it. Any one, who has lived long enough to note changes of the sort, must have perceived how fast men of probity and virtue are loosing their influence in the country, to be superseded by those who scarcely deem an affectation of the higher qualities necessary to their success. This fearful change must, in a great measure, be ascribed to the corruption of the publick press, which, as a whole, owes its existence to the schemes of interested political adventurers.

Those who are little acquainted with the world are apt to imagine that a fact, or an argument, that is stated publickly in print, is entitled to more credit and respect than the same fact or argument presented orally, or in conversation. So far from this being true, however, in regard to the press of this country, it would be safer to infer the very reverse. Men who are accustomed daily to throw off their mistatements, become reckless of the consequences, and he who would hesitate about committing himself by an allegation made face to face, and as it were on his personal responsibility, would indite a paragraph, behind the impersonality of his editorial character, to be uttered to the world in the irresponsible columns of a journal. It is seldom, in cases which admit of doubt, that men are required to speak on the moment; but, with the compositor in waiting, the time pressing, and the moral certainty that a rival establishment will circulate the questionable statement if he decline, the editor too often throws himself into the breach. The contradiction of to-day, will make a paragraph, as well as the lie of yesterday, though he who sees the last and not the first, unless able to appreciate the character of his authority, carries away an untruth.

Instead of considering the editor of a newspaper, as an abstraction, with no motive in view but that of maintaining principles and disseminating facts, it is necessary to remember that he is a man, with all the interests and passions of one who has chosen this means to advance his fortunes, and of course, with all the accompanying temptations to abuse his opportunities, and this too, usually, with the additional drawback of being a partisan in politics, religion, or literature. If the possession of power, in ordinary cases, is a constant inducement to turn it to an unjust profit, it is peculiarly so in the extraordinary case of the control of a public press.

Editors praise their personal friends, and abuse their enemies in print, as private individuals praise their friends, and abuse their enemies with their tongues. Their position increases the number of each, and the consequence is, that the readers obtain inflated views of the first and unjust notions of the last.

If newspapers are useful in overthrowing tyrants it is only to establish a tyranny of their own. The press tyrannizes over publick men, letters, the arts, the stage, and even over private life. Under the pretence of protecting publick morals, it is corrupting them to the core, and under the semblance of maintaining liberty, it is gradually establishing a despotism as ruthless, as grasping, and one that is quite as vulgar as that of any christian state known. With loud professions of freedom of opinion, there is no tolerance; with a parade of patriotism, no sacrifice of interests; and with fulsome panegyrics on propriety, too frequently, no decency.

There is but one way of extricating the mind from the baneful influence of the press of this country, and that is by making a rigid analysis of its nature and motives. By remembering that all statements that involve disputed points are *ex parte*; that there is no impersonality, except in professions; that all the ordinary passions and interests act upon its statements with less than ordinary responsibilities; and that there is the constant temptation to abuse, which ever accompanies power, one may come, at last, to a just appreciation of its merits, and in a degree, learn to neutralize its malignant influence. But this is a freedom of mind that few attain, for few have the means of arriving at these truths!

The admixture of truth and falsehood in the intelligence circulated by the press, is one of the chief causes of its evils. A journal that gave utterance to nothing but un-truths, would loose its influence with its character, but there are none so ignorant as not to see the necessity of occasion-ally issuing truths. It is only in cases in which the editor has a direct interest to the contrary, in which he has not the leisure or the means of ascertaining facts, or in which he is himself misled by the passions, cupidity and interests of others, that untruths find a place in his columns. Still these instances may, perhaps, include a majority of the cases.

In a country like this, it is indispensable to mental inde-pendence, that every man should have a clear perception of the quality of the political news, and of the political opinions circulated by the press, for, he who confides im-plicitly to its statements is yielding himself blindly to either the designed and exaggerated praises of friends, or to the calculated abuse of opponents. As no man is either as good, or as bad, as vulgar report makes him, we can, at once, see the value that ought to be given to such statements.

All representations that dwell wholly on merits, or on faults, are to be distrusted, since none are perfect, and it may, perhaps, be added, none utterly without some redeem-ing qualities.

Whenever the papers unite to commend, without qualifi-cation, it is safe to believe in either venality, or a disposition to defer to a preconceived notion of excellence, most men choosing to float with the current, rather than to resist it, when no active motive urges a contrary course, feeding false-hood, because it flatters a predilection; and whenever cen-sure is general and sweeping, one may be almost certain it is exaggerated and false.

Puffs, political, literary, personal and national, can com-monly be detected by their *ex parte* statements, as may be their counterpart, detraction. Dishonesty of intention is easily discovered by the man of the world, in both, by the tone; and he who blindly receives either eulogium or censure, because they stand audaciously in print, demonstrates that his judgment is still in its infancy.

Authors review themselves, or friends are employed to do it for them; political adventurers have their dependants, who build their fortunes on those of their patrons; artists, players, and even religionists, are not above having recourse to such expedients to advance their interests and reputations. The world would be surprised to learn the tyranny that the press has exercised, in our own times, over some of the greatest of modern names, few men possessing the manliness and moral courage that are necessary to resist its oppression.

The people that has overturned the throne of a monarch, and set up a government of opinion in its stead, and which blindly yields its interests to the designs of those who would rule through the instrumentality of newspapers, has only exchanged one form of despotism for another.

It is often made a matter of boasting, that the United States contain so many publick journals. It were wiser to make it a cause of mourning, since the quality, in this instance, diminishes in an inverse ratio to the quantity.

Another reason may be found for the deleterious influence of the American press, in the peculiar physical condition of the country. In all communities, the better opinion, whether as relates to moral or scientific truths, tastes, manners and facts, is necessarily in the keeping of a few; the great majority of mankind being precluded by their opportunities from reaching so high in the mental scale. The proportion between the intelligent and whole numbers, after making a proper allowance on account of the differences in civilization, is probably as great in this country, as in any other; possibly it is greater among the males; but the great extent of the territory prevents its concentration, and consequently, weakens its influence. Under such circumstances, the press has less to contend with than in other countries, where designing and ignorant men would stand rebuked before the collected opinion of those who, by their characters, and information, are usually too powerful to be misled by vulgarity, sophistry and falsehood. Another reason is to be found in the popular character of the government, bodies of men requiring to be addressed in modes suited to the average qualities of masses.

In America, while the contest was for great principles, the press aided in elevating the common character, in improving the common mind, and in maintaining the common interests; but, since the contest has ceased, and the struggle has become one purely of selfishness and personal interests, it is employed, as a whole, in fast undermining its own work, and in preparing the nation for some terrible reverses, if not in calling down upon it, a just judgment of God.

As the press of this country now exists, it would seem to be expressly devised by the great agent of mischief, to depress and destroy all that is good, and to elevate and advance all that is evil in the nation. The little truth that is urged, is usually urged coarsely, weakened and rendered vicious, by personalities; while those who live by falsehoods, fallacies, enmities, partialities and the schemes of the designing, find the press the very instrument that the devils would invent to effect their designs.

A witty but unprincipled statesman of our own times, has said that 'speech was bestowed on man to conceal his thoughts;' judging from its present condition, he might have added, 'and the press to pervert truth.'

On Property

As property is the base of all civilization, its existence and security are indispensable to social improvement. Were it possible to have a community of property, it would soon be found that no one would toil, but that men would be disposed to be satisfied with barely enough for the supply of their physical wants, since none would exert themselves to obtain advantages solely for the use of others. The failure of all attempts to form communities, even on a small scale, with a common interest, goes to prove this. Where there is a rigid equality of condition, as well as of rights, that condition must necessarily be one of a low scale of mediocrity, since it is impossible to elevate those who do not possess the requisite qualities any higher. Thus we see that the societies, or religious sects, in which a community of property prevails, are content with merely supplying the wants of life, knowing little or nothing of its elegancies, refinements, or mental pleasures. These communities, moreover, possess an outlet for their idle and dissolute, by resorting to expulsion, a remedy that society itself cannot apply.

The principle of individuality, or to use a less winning term, of selfishness, lies at the root of all voluntary human exertion. We toil for food, for clothes, for houses, lands, and for property, in general. This is done, because we know that the fruits of our labor will belong to ourselves or to those who are most dear to us. It follows, that all which society enjoys beyond the mere supply of its first necessities, is dependant on the rights of property.

It is not known that man exists anywhere without establishing rules for the protection of property. Even insects, reptiles, beasts and birds, have their several possessions, in their nests, dens and supplies. So completely is animal exertion, in general, whether in man or beast, dependant on the enjoyment of this right, under limitations which mark their several conditions, that we may infer that the rights of property, to a certain extent, are founded in nature. The food obtained by this toil, cannot be taken from the mouth of man, or beast, without doing violence to one of the first of our natural rights. We apply the term of robber, or despoiler, to the reptile or bird, that preys on the aliment of another animal, as well as to the human thief. So long as natural justice is admitted to exist, the party assailed, in such cases, has a right to defend his own.

The rights of property become artificial and extended, as society becomes civilized. In the savage state the land is without owners, property consisting in the hut, the food, and the arms used in war and in the chase. In pastoral, or semi-barbarous states, use gives claims, not to individuals, but to tribes, and flocks are pastured on grounds that belong to one entire community, but to that one only. Private property is composed of cattle, sheep, tents, horses, camels, with the common claims to share in the common fields.

Civilization has established various, and in some cases, arbitrary and unjust distinctions, as pertaining to the rights of property. These are abuses, the tendency of man being to convert into curses things that Providence designed to prove benefits Still, most of the ordinances of civilized society, that are connected with this interest, are founded in reason, and ought to be rigidly maintained.

The first great principle connected with the rights of property, is its inviolability in all cases in which the laws leave it in possession of the proprietor. Every child should be taught to respect the sanctity of his neighbour's house, garden, fields and all that is his. On those parts of another's possessions, where it is permitted to go, he should go with care not to abuse the privilege, and from those parts which he is forbidden to use, he should religiously abstain. The child that is properly impressed in infancy, with the rights of property, is in little danger of committing theft in after life, or, in any other manner of invading that which is the just possession of another.

The doctrine that any one 'may do what he please with his own,' however, is false. One may do with his own, whatever the laws and institutions of his country allow, and no more. One may even respect the letter, and yet violate the spirit of those laws and institutions, committing a moral, if not a legal offence, in so doing. Thus, he, who would bring his money to bear upon the elections of a country like this, abuses his situation, unless his efforts are confined to fair and manly discussions before the body of the people.

In nations where the mass have no political rights, means have been found to accumulate power by the aid of wealth. The pretence has been that none but the rich have a stake in society. Every man who has wants, feelings, affections and character, has a stake in society. Of the two, perhaps, the necessities of men are a greater corrective of political abuses, than their surplus means. Both may lead to evil, beyond a doubt, but, as laws which are framed by all, must be tolerably impartial and general in their operation, less danger arises from the rule of the former, than from the rule of the latter. When property rules, it rules alone; but when the poor are admitted to have a voice in government, the rich are never excluded. Such is the nature of man, that all exclusive power is uniformly directed to exclusive purposes. Property always carries with it a portion of indirect political influence, and it is unwise, and even dangerous, to strengthen this influence by adding to it constitutional privileges; the result always being to make the strong stronger, and the weak weaker.

On the other hand, all who love equal justice, and, indeed, the safety of free institutions, should understand that property has its rights, and the necessity of rigidly respecting them. It is the right of the possessor of property to be placed on an equal footing with all his fellow citizens, in every respect. If he is not to be exalted on account of his wealth, neither is he to be denounced. In this country, it is the intention of the institutions, that money should neither increase nor lessen political influence.

There are habits that belong to every condition of life. The man of hereditary wealth, is usually a man of leisure, and he little understands the true spirit of democracy, who supposes that such a man is not to enjoy the tastes and inclinations, which are the fruits of leisure and cultivation, without let or hindrance. Democracy leaves every man the master of his acts and time, his tastes and habits, so long as he discharges his duty to the publick, and respects the laws. He who declaims against another for holding himself aloof from general association, arrogates to himself a power of censure that he does not rightly possess, and betrays his own consciousness of inferiority. Men of really high social station never make this complaint, for they are above jealousy; and they who do, only discover a feeling that is every way removed from the manliness and spirit of true independence.

One may certainly be purse-proud, and of all the sources of human pride, mere wealth is the basest and most vulgar minded. Real gentlemen are almost invariably above this low feeling, and they who attribute habits, that have their rise in sentiment, tastes, knowledge and refinement, to such a cause, usually make the mistake of letting their own ignorance of the existence of motives so elevated, be known. In a word, if the man of property has no more personal legal immunities than the man who has none, neither has he fewer. He is privileged to use his own means, under the general regulations of society, in the pursuit of his own happiness, and they who would interfere with him, so far from appreciating liberty, are ignorant of its vital principles.

If left to itself, unsupported by factitious political aid, but sufficiently protected against the designs and rapacity of the dishonest, property is an instrument of working most of the good that society enjoys. It elevates a national character, by affording the means of cultivating knowledge and the tastes; it introduces all above barbarism into society; and it encourages and sustains laudable and useful efforts in individuals. Like every other great good, its abuses are in proportion to its benefits.

The possessor of property is not, half the time, as much the object of envy as the needy imagine, for its corrupting influence endangers eternal peace. Great estates are generally of more benefit to the community than to their owners. They bring with them anxiety, cares, demands, and, usually, exaggerated notions, on the part of the publick, of the duties of the rich. So far from being objects of envy, their possessors are oftener the subjects of commiseration; he who has enough for his rational wants, agreeably to his habits and education, always proving the happier man.

The possessions of new families are commonly exaggerated in the publick mind, while those of long established families are as commonly diminished.

A people that deems the possession of riches its highest source of distinction, admits one of the most degrading of all influences to preside over its opinions. At no time, should money be ever ranked as more than a means, and he who lives as if the acquisition of property were the sole end of his existence, betrays the dominion of the most sordid, base, and grovelling motive, that life offers.

Property is desirable as the ground work of moral independence, as a means of improving the facilities, and of doing good to others, and as the agent in all that distinguishes the civilized man from the savage.

Property has been made the test of political rights, in two distinct forms. It has been *represented*, and it has been established as a *qualification*. The *representation* of property is effected in two modes; first, by giving the proprietor more votes than one, according to the number and situation of his freeholds; and, secondly, by raising the test of qualification so high, as to exclude all but the affluent from the franchise. The first was the English system, previously to the rent changes; the last, is the actual system of France.

A government founded on the representation of property, however direct or indirect, is radically vicious, since it is a union of two of the most corrupting influences to which man is subject. It is the proper business of government to resist the corruptions of money, and not to depend on them.

To a qualification of property, if placed so low as to embrace the great majority of the people, there is no very serious objection, though better tests might, perhaps, be devised. Residence, character, information, and fixed relations with society, ought to be added to this qualification; and it might be better, even, could they be made entirely to supersede it. In local governments, or those of towns and villages, which do little more than control property, a low property qualification is the true test of the franchise, though even in these cases, it might be well to add information and character.

On Universal Suffrage

THERE is no more a literal universal suffrage, than a literal equality. All these terms must be received in a limited sense, their meaning amounting merely to a comparison with other and older conditions of society. One half of every population is excluded from the suffrage on account of sex, and more than half of the remainder on account of age. From the class that these two great rules do not affect, another, but a small portion, is excluded for their extreme poverty, their crimes, a want of residence or as vagabonds, or for some other cause. The most popularly governed of the American states admit these doctrines.

The policy of adopting a suffrage as wide as that which is commonly called universal, has been much and plausibly contested. Better political tests, perhaps, might be applied than those which now exist, and there can be little doubt that the present system is carried too far in its application and under the particular circumstances of the country, if not too far as a general principle.

The governments of towns and villages, for instance, are almost entirely directed to the regulation of property, and to the control of local interests. In such governments universal suffrage is clearly misplaced, for several grave and obvious reasons, a few of which shall be mentioned.

Towns and villages having no legislative control over the greater interests, such as the general protection of life, the person, the character, and property, there is neither the same necessity for, nor the same justice in, letting in all classes to participate in power. The laws which control the great and predominant interests, or those which give a complexion to society, emanate from the states, which may well enough possess a wide political base. But towns and villages regulating property chiefly, there is a peculiar propriety in excluding those from the suffrage who have no immediate local interests in them. An undue proportion of the dissolute, unsettled, vicious and disorganizing, collect in towns, and that balance of society, which, under other circumstances, might neutralize their influence, is destroyed, leaving, as a consequence, the power to control their governments, under a suffrage that is universal, in the hands of the worst part of community; for, though these persons may not be in sufficient force absolutely to elevate men of their own class to office, they hold a balance between conflicting parties, uniformly act together, and commonly in favor of those who are most disposed to sacrifice principle to expediency. A system must be radically wrong, when the keeper of a tavern, or of a grocery, through his facilities in humoring one of the worst of our vices, can command more votes than a man of the highest attainments, or of the highest character.

The great immigration of foreigners into the country, and the practice of remaining, or of assembling, in the large towns, renders universal suffrage doubly oppressive to the citizens of the latter. The natives of other countries bring with them the prejudices of another and an antagonist state of society; or what is still worse, their reaction; and it is a painful and humiliating fact, that several of the principal places of this country, are, virtually, under the control of men of this class, who have few convictions of liberty, beyond those which arise from a love of licentiousness, who are totally ignorant of its governing principles, and who, in their hearts and language, are hostile to the very people whose hospitality they enjoy. Many of these men cannot even speak the language of the land, and perhaps a majority of them cannot read the great social compact, by which society is held together. Whatever may be said, on general principles, of the necessity of giving to a government the broadest possible base, few will contend that circumstances like these, ought not to qualify the regulation in practice.

Local and limited governments, like those of towns and villages, are best managed in the hands of men who have permanent and fixed interests within their boundaries, and there is little propriety in admitting the more floating part of the population to a participation of an authority that scarcely controls a single right which affects transient persons.

Universal suffrage, in the more extended sense, cannot be received as a naked proposition, without reference to facts. Some nations are totally unqualified to exercise this trust, intelligently and safely, while in others, it may be the best and more sure foundation of society. As a general rule it would be highly dangerous, though the communities that can safely bear it are to be envied and esteemed.

Systems are to be appreciated by their general effects, and not by particular exceptions. Principles also become modified in practice, by facts, and universal suffrage presents very different results in one state of society, from that which it presents in another. So long as the laboring classes of a country can receive high wages, the love of independence that is natural to man, will induce them to give their votes according to their own interests, pleasure, judgment, passions or caprices; for these are equally governing motives of human actions; but when the pressure of society shall become so great as to compel the man of small means to depend on the man of large for his comforts, or even for his bread, as is the natural tendency of all civilized society, the power of money will probably be felt adversely under a suffrage that includes all, or as nearly so, as is practicable. It may then become necessary to liberty, itself, to limit the suffrage.

The representative will necessarily have a direct moral relation to his constituency. In a community that contains many men of character and intelligence, the representation will be of a higher order, than in a community that contains few. We are not to judge of the general effects of the American system, therefore, by the present condition of its representation, though those who have the best means of observation, are of opinion that it will even now sustain a favorable comparison with that of any other country.

There are periods in the histories of all countries, in which entire nations may be said to be on their good behavior. These are the times of struggles and changes, when attention is drawn to the acts of publick men, and principles have unusual influence. Such was the case at the commencement of the American revolution; at one period of the French; and is, in a degree, the present state of the British parliament. At such periods, the same representative acts under impulses very different from those which commonly influence him, and care must be had, in comparing systems, to take into the account all the facts that would be likely to affect them.

Universal suffrage is capricious and uncertain in its minor consequences, often producing results directly contrary to those which were expected.

The transitory nature of the American population renders universal suffrage less advantageous and more injurious, than it would prove to be in a less vacillating condition of society. Thus it is, we see new men, and even strangers, filling offices in places that they entered a year previously, to quit the year that will succeed. The effect of this passing connection with a community is bad, on many accounts, but it becomes seriously so, when the floating and unstable members of society have sufficient interest to unsettle its concerns with their own fluctuating interests.

On the Publick

THERE is a disposition, under popular governments, to mistake the nature and authority of the publick. Publick opinion, as a matter of course, can only refer to that portion of the community that has cognizance of the particular circumstances it affects, but in all matters of law, of rights, and of principles, as they are connected with the general relations of society, the publick means the entire constituency, and that, too, only as it is authorized to act, by the fundamental laws, or the constitution. Thus the citizen who asserts his legal rights in opposition to the wishes of a neighborhood is not opposing the publick, but maintaining its intentions, while the particular neighborhood is arrogating to itself a power that is confided to the whole body of the state.

Tyranny can only come from the publick, in a democracy, since individuals are powerless, possessing no more rights than it pleases the community to leave in their hands. The pretence that an individual oppresses the publick, is, to the last degree, absurd, since he can do no more than exercise his rights, as they are established by law; which law is enacted, administered and interpreted by the agents of the publick.

As every man forms a portion of the publick, if honest and influenced by right principles, the citizen will be cautious how he takes sides against particular members of the community, for he is both deciding in his own case, a circumstance under which few make impartial judges, and combining with the strong to oppress the weak.

In this country, in which political authority is the possession of the body that wields opinion, influences that elsewhere counteract each other, there is a strong and dangerous
disposition to defer to the publick, in opposition to truth
and justice. This is a penalty that is paid for liberty, and it
depends on the very natural principle of flattering power. In
a monarchy, adulation is paid to the prince; in a democracy
to the people, or the publick. Neither hears the truth, as
often as is wholesome, and both suffer for the want of the
corrective. The man who resists the tyranny of a monarch,
is often sustained by the voices of those around him; but
he who opposes the innovations of the publick in a democracy, not only finds himself struggling with power, but
with his own neighbors. It follows that the oppression of
the publick is of the worst description, and all real lovers of
liberty, should take especial heed not to be accessaries to
wrongs so hard to be borne. As between the publick and
individuals, therefore, the true bias of a democrat, so far
as there is any doubt of the real merits of the controversy,
is to take sides with the latter. This is opposed to the popular
notion, which is to fancy the man who maintains his rights
against the popular will, an aristocrat, but it is none the
less true; the popular will, in cases that affect popular
pleasure, being quite as likely to be wrong, as an individual
will, in cases that affect an individual interest.

It ought to be impressed on every man's mind, in letters
of brass, *'That, in a democracy, the publick has no power
that is not expressly conceded by the institutions, and that
this power, moreover, is only to be used under the forms
prescribed by the constitution. All beyond this, is oppression,
when it takes the character of acts, and not unfrequently
when it is confined to opinion.'* Society has less need of the
corrective of publick opinion, under such a system, than
under a narrow government, for possessing all the power,
the body of the community, by framing the positive ordinances, is not compelled to check abuses by resisting, or over-

awing the laws. Great care should be had, therefore, to ascertain facts, before the citizen of a free country suffers himself to inflict the punishment of publick opinion, since it is aiding oppression in its worst form, when in error, and this too, without a sufficient object.

Another form of oppression practised by the publick, is arrogating to itself a right to inquire into, and to decide on the private acts of individuals, beyond the cognizance of the laws.

Men who have designs on the favor of the publick invite invasions on their privacy, a course that has rendered the community less scrupulous and delicate than it ought to be. All assumptions of a power to decide on conduct, that is unaccompanied by an authority to investigate facts, is adding the danger of committing rank injustice, to usurpation. The practice may make hypocrites, but it can never mend morals.

The publick, every where, is proverbially soulless. All feel when its rights, assumed or real, are invaded, but none feel its responsibilities. In republicks, the publick is, also, accused of ingratitude to its servants. This is true, few citizens of a democracy retaining the popular favor, without making a sacrifice of those principles, which conflict with popular caprices. The people, being sovereign, require the same flattery, the same humouring of their wishes, and the same sacrifices of truths, as a prince.

It is not more true, however, that the people in a democracy, are ungrateful, than that monarchs are ungrateful. The failing is common to all power, which, as a rule, is invariably as forgetful of services as it is exacting. The difference in the rewards of the servants of a prince, and the rewards of the servants of a democracy, is to be found in the greater vigilance of the first, who commonly sees the necessity of paying well. No dignities or honors conferred on a subject, moreover, can raise him to a level with his master, while a people reluctantly yield distinctions that elevate one of their own number above themselves.

In America, it is indispensable that every well wisher of true liberty should understand that acts of tyranny can only proceed from the publick. The publick, then, is to be watched, in this country, as, in other countries kings and aristocrats are to be watched.

The end of liberty is the happiness of man, and its means, that of leaving the greatest possible personal freedom of action, that comports with the general good. To supplant the exactions of the laws, therefore, by those of an unauthorized publick, is to establish restraints without the formalities and precision of legal requirements. It is putting the prejudices, provincialisms, ignorance and passions of a neighborhood in the place of statutes; or, it is establishing a power equally without general principles, and without responsibility.

Although the political liberty of this country is greater than that of nearly every other civilized nation, its personal liberty is said to be less. In other words, men are thought to be more under the control of extra-legal authority, and to defer more to those around them, in pursuing even their lawful and innocent occupations, than in almost every other country. That there is much truth in this opinion, all observant travellers agree, and it is a reproach to the moral civilization of the country that it should be so. It is not difficult to trace the causes of such a state of things, but the evil is none the less because it is satisfactorily explained. One principal reason, beyond a question, is the mistake that men are apt to make concerning the rights and powers of the publick in a popular government.

The pretence that the publick has a right to extend its jurisdiction beyond the reach of the laws, and without regard to the principles and restraints of the fundamental compact that binds society together, is, indeed, to verify the common accusation of the enemies of democracy, who affirm that, by substituting this form of government for that of a despotism, people are only replacing one tyrant by many. This saying is singularly false as respects the political action of our institutions, but society must advance farther, the country must collect more towns, a denser population, and possess a higher degree of general civilization, before it can be as confidently pronounced that it is untrue as respects the purely social.

The disgraceful desire to govern by means of mobs, which has lately become so prevalent, has arisen from misconceiving the rights of the publick. Men know that the publick, or the community, rules, and becoming impatient of any evil that presses on them, or which they fancy presses on them, they overstep all the forms of law, overlook deliberation and consultation, and set up their own local interests, and not unfrequently their passions, in the place of positive enactments and the institutions. It is scarcely predicting more than the truth will warrant, to say, that if this substitution of the caprices, motives and animosities of a portion of the publick, for the solemn ordinances of the entire legal publick, should continue, even those well affected to a popular government, will be obliged to combine with those who wish its downfall, in order to protect their persons and property, against the designs of the malevolent; for no civilized society can long exist, with an active power in its bosom that is stronger than the law.

On Deportment

MUCH of the pleasure of social communication depends on the laws of deportment. Deportment may be divided into that, which, by marking refinement and polish, is termed breeding; and that, which, though less distinguished for finesse and finish, denoting a sense of civility and respect, is usually termed manners. The first can only be expected in men and women of the world, or those who are properly styled gentlemen and ladies; while an absence of the last is a proof of vulgarity and coarseness, that every citizen of a free state should be desirous of avoiding. Breeding is always pleasant, though often arbitrary in its rules; but manners are indispensable to civilization. It is just as unreasonable to expect high breeding in any but those who are trained to it, from youth upward, as it would be to expect learning without education; but a tone of manners, that shall mark equally self-respect and a proper regard for others, is as easily acquired as reading and writing.

The gentleman should aim at a standard of deportment that is refined by sentiment and taste, without the sickliness of overstrained feelings; and those beneath him in condition, at a manly humanity, that shall not pretend to distinctions the party does not comprehend, while it carefully respects all the commoner observances of civilized intercourse.

A refined simplicity is the characteristic of all high bred deportment, in every country, and a considerate humanity should be the aim of all beneath it.

On American Deportment

THE American people are superior in deportment, in several particulars, to the people of Europe, and inferior in others. The gentlemen have less finesse, but more frankness of manner, while the other classes have less vulgarity and servility, relieved by an agreeable attention to each other's rights, and to the laws of humanity in general. On the whole, the national deportment is good, without being polished, supplying the deficiency in this last essential, by great kindness and civility. In that part of deportment which affects the rights of all, such as the general and common laws of civility, the absence of social selfishness, and a strict regard to the wants and feebleness of woman, all other nations might be benefitted by imitating this.

The defects in American deportment are, notwithstanding, numerous and palpable. Among the first, may be ranked insubordination in children, and a general want of respect for age. The former vice may be ascribed to the business habits of the country, which leave so little time for parental instruction, and perhaps, in some degree, to the arts of political agents, who, with their own advantage in view, among the other expedients of their cunning, have resorted to the artifice of separating children from their natural advisers, by calling meetings of the young, to decide on the fortunes and policy of the country. Every advertisement calling assemblies of the young, to deliberate on national concerns, ought to be deemed an insult to the good sense, the modesty, and the filial piety of the class to which it is addressed.

The Americans are reproached, also, with the want of a proper deference for social station; the lower classes manifesting their indifference by an unnecessary insolence. As a rule, this charge is unmerited, civility being an inherent quality of the American character; still, there are some who mistake a vulgar audacity for independence. Men and women of this disposition, require to be told that, in thus betraying their propensities, they are giving the strongest possible proofs that they are not what their idle vanity would give reason to suppose they fancy themselves, the equals of those whom they insult by their coarseness.

More of this class err from ignorance, want of reflection, or a loose habit of regulating their conduct in their intercourse with others, than from design. The following anecdote will give an instance of what is meant, and, as the circumstance related is true, the reader will perceive the ludicrous impression that is left, by these gross improprieties of behaviour. A gentleman, who shall be called Winfield, perceiving a girl of eight or ten years of age, endeavoring to find an entrance to his house, enquired her errand. 'I have some hats for *Winfield's girls,*' was the answer. Although shocked at this rudeness, Mr Winfield told the child, that by going to a certain door, she would find a servant to receive her. 'Oh!' replied the girl, 'I have already seen the *Irish lady*, in the kitchen.' This Irish *lady*, was the cook, a very good woman in her way, but one who had no pretensions to be so termed!

Such a confusion in the ideas of this child, is a certain proof of a want of training, for the young ladies who were treated so disrespectfully, were not the less ladies, nor did the cook become more than a cook, for the vulgarity. Facts are not to be changed by words, and all they obtain, who fancy their language and deportment can alter the relations of society, is an exposure of their own ignorance.

The entire complexion, and in many respects, the well being of society, depends on the deportment of its different members, to each other. It behoves the master to be kind to the servant, the servant to be respectful and obedient to his master; the young and inexperienced to defer to the aged and experienced; the ignorant to attend to the admonitions of the wise, and the unpolished to respect the tastes and habits of the refined.

In other countries, where positive ordinances create social distinctions in furtherance of these ends, it is believed they cannot be obtained in any other manner; but it is to be hoped that America is destined to prove, that common sense and the convictions of propriety and fitness, are as powerful agents as force. The servility and arrogance of a highly artificial social scale are not to be desired, but, having positive social facts, also, which cannot be dispensed with, it is vain to resist them. Civility and respect, are the sure accompaniments of a high civilization, and the admission of obvious facts is an indispensable requisite of common sense, as their denial is evidence of infatuation and folly.

There is a moral obligation in every man to conduct himself with civility to all around him. Neither are his particular notions of what is proper, to be taken as an excuse for his rudeness and insults. Refinement and the finesse of breeding are not expected from the majority, but none are so ignorant, in this country, as not to distinguish between what is proper and what is improper in deportment.

Some men imagine they have a right to ridicule what are termed 'airs,' in others. If it could be clearly established what are 'airs,' and what not, a corrective of this sort might not be misapplied. But the term is conventional, one man experiencing disgust at what enters into the daily habits of another. It is exceedingly hazardous, therefore, for any but those who are familiar with the best usages of the world, to pronounce any thing 'airs,' because it is new to them, since what has this appearance to such persons may be no more than a proof of cultivation and of a good tone of manners.

On the other hand, many who have been thrown accidentally and for short periods, into the society of the more refined classes, adopt their usages without feeling or understanding their reasons and advantages, caricaturing delicacy and sentiment, and laying stress on habits, which, though possibly convenient in themselves, are not deemed at all essential by men and women of the world. These affectations of breeding are laughed at, as the 'silver-forkisms' of pretenders. To the man of the world it is unnecessary to point out the want of taste in placing such undue stress on these immaterial things, but it may not be unnecessary to the novice in the usages of the better circles, to warn him that his ignorance will be more easily seen by his exaggerations, than by his deficiencies of manner. The Duc de Richlieu is said to have detected an impostor by his *not* taking olives with his fingers.

But these are points of little interest with the mass, while civility and decency lie at the root of civilization. There is no doubt that, in general, America has retrograded in manners within the last thirty years. Boys and even men, wear their hats in the houses of all classes, and before persons of all ages and conditions. This is not independence, but vulgarity, for nothing sooner distinguishes a gentleman from a blackguard, than the habitual attention of the former to the minor civilities established by custom. It has been truly said, that the man who is well dressed respects himself more, and behaves himself better, than the man that is ill dressed; but it is still more true that the man who commences with a strict observance of the commoner civilities, will be the most apt to admit of the influence of refinement on his whole character.

On Publick Opinion

PUBLICK opinion is the lever by which all things are moved, in a democracy. It has even become so powerful in monarchies, as, virtually, to destroy despotism in all really civilized countries, holding in check the will and passions of princes.

Publick opinion, however, like all things human, can work evil in proportion to its power to do good. On the same principle that the rebound is proportioned to the blow in physics, there can be no moral agent capable of benefitting man that has not an equal power to do him harm. Publick opinion rightly directed is the highest source of national virtue, as publick opinion, which has taken a wrong direction, is the surest means of serving the devil.

In a democracy, as a matter of course, every effort is made to seize upon and create publick opinion, which is, substantially, securing power. One of the commonest arts practised, in connection with this means of effecting objects, is to simulate the existence of a general feeling in favor, or against, any particular man, or measure; so great being the deference paid to publick opinion, in a country like this, that men actually yield their own sentiments to that which they believe to be the sentiment of the majority.

In politics, however, and, indeed, in all other matters that are of sufficient magnitude to attract general attention, there are adverse sentiments, which, were it not for the absurdity of the phrase, might almost be termed two publick opinions. This is the result of party feeling which induces men to adopt in gross, the prejudices, notions and judgments of the particular faction to which they belong, often without examination, and generally without candor. When two men of equal intelligence, of the same means of ascertaining facts, and of the same general fairness of disposition, hold the opposite extremes of opinion on the character of a particular individual, or of a particular measure, we see the extent to which a bias may be carried, and the little value that those who wish only to support the truth ought to attach even to publick opinion, in matters that will admit of doubt.

As no reparation can ever be made, in this world, to the individual who has been wronged by publick opinion, all good men are cautious how they listen to accusations that are unsupported by testimony, vulgar report being more likely to be wrong than to be right.

In matters that admit of investigation and proof, publick opinion in the end, when passion, prejudice and malice have had their day, is very apt to come to a just decision, but this is often too late to repair the wrong done to the sufferer. In matters that, by their nature, cannot be clearly established, artifice, the industry of the designing, and studied misrepresentations, permanently take the place of facts, history itself being, as a whole, but an equivocal

relation of all the minor events, and a profound mystification as to motives.

Publick opinion will be acted on in this country, by its
enemies, as the easiest and most effectual mode of effecting
their purposes, bodies of men never being sufficiently clear-
sighted to detect remote consequences. It is said to be a
common practice in Europe, for the governments to incite
commotions, when they wish to alarm the country on the
subject of any particular opinion, as the surest and promp-
test method of checking its advance. The excesses of the
French revolution are now attributed to the schemes of
agents of this sort; the opponents of liberty finding it impossible to stem the torrent, having recourse to the opposite
policy of pushing it into revolting extremes.

Excitement is a word that, as regards the publick in a
country like this, ought to be expunged from its dictionary.
In full possession of the power, there is every motive for
deliberation and enquiry on the part of the people, and
every inducement to abstain from undue agitation. 'Excitement,' may favor the views of selfish individuals, but it can
never advance the interests of truth. All good citizens should
turn a deaf ear to every proposal to aid in producing an
'excitement,' as it is calling into existence a uniform enemy
of reason, and the most certain agent of defeating the intention of the institutions, which are based on investigation and
common sense.

Whenever the government of the United States shall
break up, it will probably be in consequence of a false
direction having been given to publick opinion. This is the
weak point of our defences, and the part to which the
enemies of the system will direct all their attacks. Opinion
can be so perverted as to cause the false to seem the true; the
enemy, a friend, and the friend, an enemy; the best interests
of the nation to appear insignificant, and trifles of moment;
in a word, the right the wrong, and the wrong the right.

In a country where opinion has sway, to seize upon it,

is to seize upon power. As it is a rule of humanity that the upright and well intentioned are comparatively passive, while the designing, dishonest and selfish are the most untiring in their efforts, the danger of publick opinion's getting a false direction, is fourfold, since few men think for themselves. Perhaps there is not, in all America, apart from general principles, a sentiment that is essentially just, and which is recognized as publick opinion; a sufficient proof of which is to be found in the fact that publick opinion is constantly vibrating around truth, which alone is unchangeable.

Publick opinion has got a wrong, if not a dangerous direction, already, in this country, on several essential points. It has a fearfully wrong direction on the subject of the press, which it sustains in its tyranny and invasions on private rights, violating all sanctity of feeling, rendering men indifferent to character, and, indeed, rendering character itself of little avail, besides setting up an irresponsible and unprincipled power that is stronger than the government itself. One of its consequences is a laxity of opinion on the subject of wrongs committed by the press, that amounts to a denial of justice. Another, and a still graver result, is to give an unrestrained supremacy to an engine that is quite as able, and perhaps more likely, to corrupt and destroy society than to reform it. This fearful state of things, which is better adapted than any other, to restrain good, and to prefer bold and bad men, has been brought about by the action of the press, itself, on publick opinion, and is an example of the manner in which this tremendous agent can be perverted to evil, in a popular government. It follows, that publick opinion should be watched and protected from receiving a wrong bias, as we would protect and overlook the first impressions of a child.

Publick opinion in America is exposed to another danger, growing out of the recent colonial origin of the country. There is no question that the people of this country defer in an unusual manner to foreign opinions, more particularly to those of the nation from which they are derived. The proof of this is ample, but one may constantly see quotations from English journals, in support of the pretensions of politicians, writers, artists, and all others, who are liable to the decisions of their fellow citizens for the estimation in which they are held. An opinion is seldom given in Europe of any thing American, unless from impure motives. The country attracts too little attention in the other hemisphere, to be included in the ordinary comments of the civilized world. There are, and may be, an occasional exception, but this is the rule. As many of the interests of this country are opposed to the interests of European nations, efforts are constantly made to influence opinion here, in favor of interests there. The doctrine of free trade, as it is called, has this origin, having been got up by English writers, to prevent other states from resorting to the same expedients to foster industry, that have so well succeeded in Great Britain. The factitious condition of all things in that great empire, renders any derangement hazardous, and while America trifles with her welfare, like a vigorous youth who is careless of his health through reliance on his constitution, England watches over every material concern with the experience, vigilance and distrust of age. Hence it is that every means is resorted to, to extol men who have become the dupes of English sophistry, and to depreciate those who resist her schemes.

We have lately seen, on the part of France, an open and a direct attempt to interfere between the people and the government, in an affair touching the character and highest interests of the country, and although the appeal injured the cause of those who urged it, by exposing their sophistry and bad faith, it proves the reliance that foreign powers have on their ability to influence publick opinion, here, even in matters touching our own dearest interests!

Another familiar and recent instance of the efforts of

foreigners to influence American opinion, may be cited in connection with the late quarrel with France. It is known that the English government mediated to prevent a war. This mediation was accepted on the part of the American government, with the express reservation that France must comply with the terms of the treaty. In other words, we merely conditioned to delay acting, until the effort should be made to induce France to comply with all we asked. France saw reasons to change her policy, and to comply with our terms, before the acceptance of the English mediation was known, and yet strong efforts have been made to persuade the American people that the accommodation was produced through English mediation, and that England was pledged to see this accommodation effected, in the character of an arbitrator. The first is untrue as to fact, and the last is opposed to all the principles of arbitration, as nothing was placed at the decision of the English government. The case is a recent proof of the vigilance that is necessary to keep publick opinion independent of foreign domination.

Opinion is the moving power of this country, and it would be extreme weakness to suppose that other nations, which are ever ready to lavish their treasure and to shed their blood, in order to effect their purposes, would neglect means so sure, easy and noiseless, as that of acting on the common mind. The danger of evil from this source will increase with the growing power of the country, or, as her policy will be likely to influence foreign interests, in a ratio proportioned to her strength and wealth.

No nation can properly boast of its independence while its opinion is under the control of foreigners, and least of all, a nation with institutions dependant on the popular will.

On Civilization

CIVILIZATION means a condition of society that is the opposite of the savage, or barbarous state. In other languages this term is more strictly applied to the arts of life, than in the English, in which we are more apt to associate with it the moral condition of a country.

England stands at the head of modern civilization, as a whole, although many countries surpass her in particular parts. The higher tastes of England are not as refined and cultivated, perhaps, as those of Italy and France, but the base of society is infinitely more advanced.

America occupies a middle place in the scale, wanting most of the higher tastes, and excelling in that species of civilization which marks ease and improvement in the middling and lower classes. There is one feature connected with the civilization of this country that is peculiar; for while the people have long been accustomed to the habits of England, they have not been possessed of those arts by which the different objects of the comforts they have enjoyed are produced. For a long time articles as humble as hats, shovels and hoes, were not fabricated in the country, though the time never has been when the Anglo-Americans were unaccustomed to their use.

Although there is a difference between the civilization of the towns, and that of the country, in America, it is less marked than in Europe. The disparity between the refinement, mental cultivation and the elegances of life, is much less apparent than usual, as between an American capital and an American village, though the localities, of course, make some distinctions. As a whole, civilization, while it is less perfect in this country than in the European nations, is more equally diffused throughout the entire community. Still it better becomes the American people to strive to advance their condition than to manifest a weak, unmanly and provincial sensibility to the faults that are occasionally commented on, nations, like individuals, merely betraying a consciousness of their own demerits, by meeting admonition with insult and anger.

The Americans are deficient on many points of civilization, solely for the want of physical force in given places, the practice of covering large surfaces unavoidably retarding the improvements of the nation. This is rather the subject of regret, than a matter of reproach. They are almost ignorant of the art of music, one of the most elevating, innocent and refining of human tastes, whose influence on the habits and morals of a people is of the most beneficial tendency. This taste and knowledge are not only wanting to the people, but an appreciation of their importance. They are also wanting in most of the high tastes, and consequently in the high enjoyments, that accompany a knowledge of all the fine arts in general, and in much that depends on learning, research, and familiarity with the world.

The Americans excel in humanity, in the ordinary comforts, though inferior to the English in this respect, in general civility, in the means of motion while confined to great routes, in shipping and most of the facilities of trade, in common instruction and an aptitude to ordinary pursuits, and in an absence of the sophisms that beset older and more artificial systems. It is, however, to be regretted, that as the nation recedes from the struggle that created the present system, the truths that come uppermost in the collision, are gradually yielding to a new set of sophisms, more peculiar to the present order of things.

There is a familiar and too much despised branch of civilization, of which the population of this country is singularly and unhappily ignorant; that of cookery. The art of eating and drinking, is one of those on which more depends, perhaps, than on any other, since health, activity of mind, constitutional enjoyments, even learning, refinements, and, to a certain degree, morals, are all, more or less, connected with our diet. The Americans are the grossest feeders of any civilized nation known. As a nation, their food is heavy, coarse, ill prepared and indigestible, while it is taken in the least artificial forms that cookery will allow. The predominance of grease in the American kitchen, coupled with the habits of hasty eating and of constant expectoration, are the causes of the diseases of the stomach so common in America. The science of the table extends far beyond the indulgence of our appetites, as the school of manners includes health and morals, as well as that which is agreeable. Vegetable diet is almost converted into an injury in America, from an ignorance of the best modes of preparation, while even animal food is much abused, and loses half its nutriment.

The same is true as respects liquors. The heating and exciting wines, the brandies, and the coarser drinks of the laboring classes, all conspire to injure the physical and the moral man, while they defeat their own ends.

These are points of civilization on which this country has yet much to learn, for while the tables of the polished and cultivated partake of the abundance of the country, and wealth has even found means to introduce some knowledge of the kitchen, there is not perhaps on the face of the globe, the same number of people among whom the good things of the earth are so much abused, or ignorantly wasted, as among the people of the United States. National character is, in some measure, affected by a knowledge of the art of preparing food, there being as good reason to suppose that man is as much affected by diet as any other animal, and it is certain that the connection between our moral and physical qualities is so intimate as to cause them to react on each other.

On the Right of Petition

THE right of petition is guarantied to the American citizen by an amendment to the constitution, made in 1801. By this clause, *congress* is prohibited from passing any law to prevent the *people* from *peaceably assembling*, in order to petition the government for a redress of grievances. This prohibition, like those on the subjects of the liberty of the press, liberty of speech and liberty of conscience, was perfectly supererogatory, the states having conceded to congress no authority to pass any law to the contrary. It is understood that all these provisions were introduced through the influence of Mr Jefferson, who was desirous that the constitution should exhibit on its face, what might be termed its profession of political faith, since foreigners did not comprehend the negative restrictions on the power of the federal government, that grow out of the fact of its being purely a government of deputed and defined authority.

The right of petition is by no means an important political right in this country, where the constituents hold so strong a check on their representatives, and where no important laws can long exist without their approbation. In countries in which the people cannot assemble to cause publick opinion to act on their rulers, and in which the great majority are disfranchised, or never possessed a vote, the right of petition is an all important right. Men confound the characters of the institutions of different nations, when they ascribe the same importance to it here.

Although the people have a right to petition, congress is not bound to waste its time in listening to and in discussing the matter of opinions, on the merits of which that body has already decided. A discretionary power rests in congress to receive, or to reject a petition, at pleasure, the right going no farther than the assembling and petitioning; else would it be in the power of a small proportion of the people to occupy all the time of the national legislature on vexatious and useless questions.

A state has no right to petition congress at all. The legislature of a state has its limited powers as well as congress, and, did the constitution of a particular state include this among the other powers of its legislature, the governing principle of the federal constitution is opposed to it. The right of petition as claimed by a state can do no legitimate good, and may lead to much evil, as a brief examination will show. The federal government acts directly on the people, through agents of its own; for whenever it accepts the agency of a state, the agents of that state are in effect the agents of the general government. Now, the representation in one body of congress, is not a state representation, but it is a representation founded on numbers. As a state, if possessing authority to petition, one state ought to have the weight of another, whereas, in congress, one state has much more influence than another, as the following example will show. The senators of fourteen states may vote for the passage, or the repeal of a law, under the influence of petitions from their several state legislatures, and yet the veto of the representatives of the remaining twelve states shall defeat the measure in the other house. It follows that the states, purely as states, are not so strictly constituents of congress as to claim a *right* to petition. The danger of the practice is derived from the tendency of creating local feelings, through the agency of the local governments, and of thus endangering the peace of the Union.

It would be difficult to show that a state has more right to petition congress, than congress has to petition a state. This interference of the different parts of a complicated and nicely balanced machine, might derange its entire movement.

On Commerce

COMMERCE, in a general sense, is trade, but it is also usual to apply the word particularly to the traffick between nations. Navigation is not commerce, but a means of conducting commerce.

Commerce is merely an incident of civilized society, though there is always a strong disposition in commercial communities to treat it as a principal. The interests of commerce, in a general sense, depend on certain great principles, which ought always to be respected; but, as these interests, by their nature, are also liable to be influenced by the constant vicissitudes arising out of the fluctuations of trade, there is a strong disposition in those connected with commerce, to sacrifice all governing rules, to protect the interests of the day. This disposition is common to man, but it is more active in merchants, on account of the magnitude and precarious nature of the risks they run. The agriculturist who loses a crop, suffers an injury, more or less serious, that another year will repair; but the merchant who loses his adventures, is usually ruined.

It follows, that a community governed by men in trade, or which is materially influenced by men in trade, is governed without any fixed principles, every thing being made to yield to the passing interests of the hour, those interests being too engrossing to admit of neglect, or postponement.

It is a mistake to suppose commerce favorable to liberty. Its tendency is to a monied aristocracy, and this, in effect, has always been the polity of every community of merchants. Commerce is an enemy of despotic power in the hands of a prince, of church influence, and of hereditary aristocracies, from which facts it has obtained its reputation of sustaining freedom; but, as a class, merchants will always be opposed to the control of majorities.

The true office of commerce is to facilitate exchanges of articles between men, to the amount that their wants and interests require; but as every transfer of property leaves a profit with the merchant, he has a disposition to increase his gains, by pushing his transactions beyond the just limits of trade. This disposition is best checked by the penalties of bankruptcies, but, in a country like this, in which no such penalty exists, the consequence is to produce an unbroken succession of commercial reverses, that affect the value of all the property in the nation, almost periodically.

Commerce is entitled to a complete and efficient protection in all its legal rights, but the moment it presumes to control a country, or to substitute its fluctuating expedients for the high principles of natural justice that ought to lie at the root of every political system, it should be frowned on, and rebuked.

The merchant who is the immediate agent in paying the duties on goods, has no more claims than another, as the money eventually comes from the pocket of the consumer, and the factor is amply paid for his services in his profits.

All legislation affecting the currency, commerce and banking, in a country like this, ought to be limited, as far as circumstances will allow, to general and simple provisions, the nature of the institutions forbidding the interference that is elsewhere practised with advantage. A familiar example will show our meaning. In all commercial communities there is a commercial mart, or a capital, where exchanges are affected, cargoes disposed of in gross, and where all the great interests of trade concentrate, as the blood flows to and from the heart. In identified governments, like that of England, for instance, legislation may respect this natural tendency to concentration in commerce, and enact laws for its especial benefit and protection. Thus an English law may have an especial relation to the interests of London, as the mart that regulates the entire currency of the kingdom. But, on the other hand, in a government like that of America, there is a principle of diffusion, which requires that the legislation should be general in its application. New York and New Orleans for instance, regulate the currency and exchanges of the whole country; but congress cannot pass a law to aid these legitimate efforts of trade, since any legislation that should favor New York at the expense of Philadelphia, in appearances even, would be opposed to the controlling principle of the compact. It follows, that the interference of the government with all such questions, in this country, should be unfrequent and cautious, since it possesses a power to injure, with very little power to benefit.

The real merchant is a man of a high pursuit, and has need of great general knowledge, much firmness of character, and of far-sighted views, to succeed in his objects. He is a principal agent in extending knowledge and civilization, and is entitled to a distinguished place in the scale of human employments. But the mere factor, who is the channel of communication between the producer and the consumer, in what is called a regular trade, has no more claims to this character, than the clerk who copies a treaty has a claim to be considered a negotiator.

On the Circulating Medium

NECESSITY has induced men to establish a certain standard of value, by means of the precious metals, to represent property. As it is desirable that this standard of value should fluctuate as little as possible, laws have been passed rendering it illegal to receive more than a fixed rate of interest for money. There can be no question that these laws would be singularly useful, did not dealers find means to evade them, for a variation in the value of the representative of property, renders all contracts liable to the hazards of a fluctuation, in addition to that of the article purchased. It is to be feared, however, that nothing short of making usury criminal, will ever effect this object; if, indeed, such a remedy be practicable.

As the world does not contain a sufficiency of the precious metals to represent any considerable amount of its debts, it has been found necessary to resort to a system of credits, for the purposes of commerce, that is based on gold and silver. This system is so simple, that any one can understand it. The precious metals have a currency throughout christendom, while the credit of an individual, or of a banking institution, is limited. All that is required of the two latter, therefore, is, that its paper should be redeemed in specie, as specie shall be wanted.

In a country like America a purely specie currency is utterly impracticable. Although money is not actually wanted for a tithe of the debts that are due, at any one moment, so much more is wanted than can be obtained in the precious metals, that a recourse to the credit system is unavoidable, as a single feature of the true condition of the country will show.

America, in the states and territories, contains about twelve hundred thousand square miles. This immense country is in the course of settlement, and the transfers of real estate, are a hundred-fold what they are in Europe, on the same extent of surface. A piece of land is frequently sold several times in the course of a single year, whereas centuries often elapse in older countries, without the sale of a given property. Every transfer of title causes an indebtedness, and consequently a necessity for a circulating medium to represent it. The earth does not probably contain a sufficiency of the precious metals, at their present value, to represent all the debts of this one country.

On the other hand, nothing is easier than to abuse a

system of credits. The unrestrained issue of paper-money, with its attendant contractions, keeps the value of property unsettled, creates pressures and bankruptcies, and otherwise produces the instability that so peculiarly marks the condition of American trade.

Specie should be the basis of all currency. There should also be enough of the precious metals floating in the community, to meet its minor daily wants, the proper office of credit being to represent money in large sums, and not to represent money in small sums. For all the purposes of payments from the pocket, nothing is so convenient, or so safe, as gold and silver, as all who have tried it well know. Indeed so palpable is the fact, that in Europe, men of wealth almost invariably use gold for this purpose, even in those countries in which it is slightly above the standard of value in price, and it may be questioned if any paper ought to be issued of a value less than fifty or a hundred dollars. In short, the precious metals are intended to circulate among those who have not the leisure nor knowledge to ascertain the credit of paper, while the credit system is to facilitate the operations of trade, and to supply the deficiency in gold and silver in the payment of larger sums. Any effort to make paper do more than legitimately belongs to its office, is an attempt to supplant the interests of society by serving the interests of money dealers.

On Slavery

DOMESTIC slavery is an institution as old as human annals, and probably will continue, in its spirit, through different modifications, as long as man shall remain under the different degrees of civilization that mark his actual existence. Slavery is no more sinful, by the christian code, than it is sinful to wear a whole coat, while another is in tatters, to eat a better meal than a neighbor, or otherwise to enjoy ease and plenty, while our fellow creatures are suffering and in want. According to the doctrines of Christ, we are 'to do as we would be done by,' but this law is not to be applied to slavery more than to any other interest of life. It is quite possible to be an excellent christian and a slave holder, and the relations of master and slave, may be a means of exhibiting some of the mildest graces of the character, as may those of king and subject, or principal and dependent, in any of the other modifications of human institutions.

In one sense, slavery may actually benefit a man, there being little doubt that the African is, in nearly all respects, better off in servitude in this country, than when living in a state of barbarism at home.

But, while slavery, in the abstract, can no more be considered a sin, than most human ordinances, it leads to sin in its consequences, in a way peculiarly its own, and may to be set down as an impolitic and vicious institution. It encourages those faults of character that depend on an uncontrolled will, on the one side, and an abject submission, on the other. It usually limits the moral existence of the slave, too, as there is a necessity of keeping him ignorant, in order that he may be held in subjection.

Slavery is of two kinds; one in which the slave is a chattel, and can be disposed of as such, and one in which he is attached to the soil, like a fixture, and can only be sold with the land. The former is the condition of the American slave; the latter the condition of the European serf. All Europe, formerly, had serfs, or slaves, of the latter class, though their existence is now confined to a few countries in the north and east of that quarter of the world. Still, the consequences of the old system are, more or less, to be traced, in most European countries, and, though differing in degree their people may as fairly be termed slaves in principle, as those of our own southern states.

On American Slavery

AMERICAN slavery is one of the most unqualified kind, considering the slave as a chattel, that is transferable at will, and in full property. The slave, however, is protected in his person to a certain extent, the power of the master to chastise and punish, amounting to no more than the parental power.

American slavery is distinguished from that of most other parts of the world, by the circumstance that the slave is a variety of the human species, and is marked by physical peculiarities so different from his master, as to render future amalgamation improbable. In ancient Rome, in modern Europe generally, and in most other countries, the slave not being thus distinguished, on obtaining his freedom, was soon lost in the mass around him; but nature has made a stamp on the American slave that is likely to prevent this consummation, and which menaces much future ill to the country. The time must come when American slavery shall cease, and when that day shall arrive, (unless early and effectual means are devised to obviate it,) two races will exist in the same region, whose feelings will be embittered by inextinguishable hatred, and who carry on their faces, the respective stamps of their factions. The struggle that will follow, will necessarily be a war of extermination. The evil day may be delayed, but can scarcely be averted.

American slavery is mild, in its general features, and physical suffering cannot properly be enumerated among its evils. Neither is it just to lay too heavy stress on the personal restraints of the system, as it is a question whether men feel very keenly, if at all, privations of the amount of which they know nothing. In these respects, the slavery of this country is but one modification of the restraints that are imposed on the majority, even, throughout most of Europe. It is an evil, certainly, but in a comparative sense, not as great an evil as it is usually imagined. There is scarcely a nation of Europe that does not possess institutions that inflict as gross personal privations and wrongs, as the slavery of America. Thus the subject is compelled to bear arms in a quarrel in which he has no real concern, and to incur the risks of demoralization and death in camps and fleets, without any crime or agency of his own. From all this, the slave is exempt, as well as from the more ordinary cares of life.

Slavery in America, is an institution purely of the states, and over which the United States has no absolute control. The pretence, however, that congress has no right to entertain the subject, is unsound, and cannot be maintained. Observing the prescribed forms, slavery can be legally abolished, by amending the constitution, and congress has power, by a vote of two thirds of both houses, to propose amendments to that instrument. Now, whatever congress has power to do, it has power to discuss; by the same rule, that it is a moral innovation on the rights of the states to discuss matters in congress, on which congress has no authority to legislate. A constitutional right, and expediency, however, are very different things. Congress has full power to declare war against all the nations of the earth, but it would be madness to declare war against even one of them, without sufficient cause. It would be equal madness for congress, in the present state of the country, to attempt to propose an amendment of the constitution, to abolish slavery altogether, as it would infallibly fail, thereby raising an irritating question without an object.

On Slavery in the District of Columbia

CONGRESS having all power to legislate for the District of Columbia, there can be no reasonable doubt of its power to legislate on slavery, as well as any other interest, under the limits of the constitution. A plausible question might even be raised whether the ordinary restrictions of the constitution apply at all to the legislation of the District, and whether the powers of congress over this particular portion of the country, are not as absolute as the powers of parliament in Great Britain.

Still the legislation for the District, in principle, depends on that general rule which ought to guide all just legislators. To pretend that a member of congress from Vermont, or a member of congress from Louisiana, is to respect the opinions of his own immediate constituents, in legislating especially for the District of Columbia, is like pretending that the emperor of Austria, who is equally sovereign of both countries, should consult the interests of the people of the kingdom of Bohemia, in establishing laws for the kingdom of Hungary. The relation between the constituent of the member and the District, is altogether anomalous, and, on no just principle, can be made to extend to this absolute control.

All legislation that is especially intended for the District, should keep the interests of the District alone in view, subject to the great reasons for which this territory was formed, and to the general principles of morality. So far as any influence beyond that of the District is concerned, on the question of slavery, this legislation should be more in the interest of the slave-holding states, than in the interests of the non-slave-holding states, as with the latter it is purely a negative question, whereas, with the former, it has a positive affirmative connection with their immediate interests, in more senses than one. Thus the slave-holder has a claim to be able to visit the seat of government, attended by his body servants, and this, too, without incurring any unpleasant risks of their loss merely to satisfy the abstract notions of right of the citizens of the non-slave-holding states. This claim may not be so great as to overshadow those of the inhabitants of the District itself, should they demand a law for the emancipation of their slaves, but is quite great enough to overshadow the negative interests of the resident of a non-slave-holding estate.

In the management of this interest, in general, it ought to be remembered, that to the citizen of the non-slave-holding state, slavery offers little more than a question of abstract principles, while to the citizen of the slave-holding state it offers a question of the highest practical importance, and one that, mis-managed, might entirely subvert the order of his social organization.

On Party

IT is commonly said that political parties are necessary to liberty. This is one of the mistaken opinions that have been inherited from those who, living under governments in which there is no true political liberty, have fancied that the struggles which are inseparable from their condition, must be common to the condition of all others.

England, the country from which this people is derived, and, until the establishment of our own form of government, the freest nation of Christendom, enjoys no other liberty than that which has been obtained by the struggles of parties. Still retaining in the bosom of the state, a power in theory, which, if carried out in practice, would effectually overshadow all the other powers of the state, it may truly be necessary to hold such a force in check, by the combinations of political parties. But the condition of America, in no respect, resembles this. Here, the base of the government is the constituencies, and its balance is in the divided action of their representatives, checked as the latter are by frequent elections. As these constituencies are popular, the result is a free, or a popular government.

Under such a system, in which fundamental laws are settled by a written compact, it is not easy to see what good can be done by parties, while it is easy to see that they may effect much harm. It is the object of this article, to point out a few of the more prominent evils that originate from such a source.

Party is known to encourage prejudice, and to lead men astray in the judgment of character. Thus it is we see one half the nation extolling those that the other half condemns, and condemning those that the other half extols. Both cannot be right, and as passions, interests and prejudices are all enlisted on such occasions, it would be nearer the truth to say that both are wrong.

Party is an instrument of error, by pledging men to support its policy, instead of supporting the policy of the state. Thus we see party measures almost always in extremes, the resistance of opponents inducing the leaders to ask for more than is necessary.

Party leads to vicious, corrupt and unprofitable legislation, for the sole purpose of defeating party. Thus have we seen those territorial divisions and regulations which ought to be permanent, as well as other useful laws, altered, for no other end than to influence an election.

Party, has been a means of entirely destroying that local independence, which elsewhere has given rise to a representation that acts solely for the nation, and which, under other systems is called the country party, every legislator being virtually pledged to support one of two opinions; or, if a shade of opinion between them, a shade that is equally fettered, though the truth be with neither.

The discipline and organization of party, are expedients to defeat the intention of the institutions, by putting managers in the place of the people; it being of little avail that a majority elect, when the nomination rests in the hands of a few.

Party is the cause of so many corrupt and incompetent men's being preferred to power, as the elector, who, in his own person, is disposed to resist a bad nomination, yields to the influence and a dread of factions.

Party pledges the representative to the support of the executive, right or wrong, when the institutions intend that he shall be pledged only to justice, expediency and the right, under the restrictions of the constitution.

When party rules the people do not rule, but merely such a portion of the people as can manage to get the control of party. The only method by which the people can completely control the country, is by electing representatives known to prize and understand the institutions; and, who, so far from being pledged to support an administration, are pledged to support nothing but the right, and whose characters are guarantees that this pledge will be respected.

The effect of party is always to supplant established power. In a monarchy it checks the king; in a democracy it controls the people.

Party, by feeding the passions and exciting personal interests, overshadows truth, justice, patriotism, and every other publick virtue, completely reversing the order of a democracy, by putting unworthy motives in the place of reason.

It is a very different thing to be a democrat, and to be a member of what is called a democratic party; for the first insists on his independence and an entire freedom of opinion, while the last is incompatible with either.

The great body of the nation has no real interest in party. Every local election should be absolutely independent of great party divisions, and until this be done, the intentions of the American institutions will never be carried out, in their excellence.

Party misleads the public minds as to the rights and duties of the citizen. An instance has recently occurred, in which a native born citizen of the United States of America, the descendant of generations of Americans, has become the object of systematic and combined persecution, because he published a constitutional opinion that conflicted with the interests and passions of party, although having no connection with party himself; very many of his bitterest assailants being foreigners, who have felt themselves authorized to pursue this extraordinary course, as the agents of party!

No freeman, who really loves liberty, and who has a just perception of its dignity, character, action and objects, will ever become a mere party man. He may have his preferences as to measures and men, may act in concert with those who think with himself, on occasions that require concert, but it will be his earnest endeavour to hold himself a free agent, and most of all to keep his mind untrammelled by the prejudices, frauds, and tyranny of factions.

On Individuality

INDIVIDUALITY is the aim of political liberty. By leaving to the citizen as much freedom of action and of being, as comports with order and the rights of others, the institutions render him truly a freeman. He is left to pursue his means of happiness in his own manner.

It is a curious circumstance, that, in endeavouring to secure the popular rights, an effect has been produced in this country totally opposed to this main object. Men have been so long accustomed to see oppression exercised in the name of one, or in the name of a few, that they have got to consider the sway of numbers as the only criterion of freedom. Numbers, however, may oppress as well as one or a few, and when such oppression occurs, it is usually of the worst character.

The habit of seeing the publick rule, is gradually accustoming the American mind to an interference with private rights that is slowly undermining the individuality of the national character. There is getting to be so much publick right, that private right is overshadowed and lost. A danger exists that the ends of liberty will be forgotten altogether in the means.

All greatness of character is dependant on individuality. The man who has no other existence than that which he partakes in common with all around him, will never have any other than an existence of mediocrity. In time, such a state of things would annihilate invention and paralyze genius. A nation would become a nation of common place labourers.

The pursuit of happiness is inseparable from the claims of individuality. To compel all to follow this object in the same manner, is to oppress all above the average tastes and information. It can only be done at the expense of that which is the aim of liberty.

An entire distinct individuality, in the social state, is neither possible nor desirable. Our happiness is so connected with the social and family ties as to prevent it; but, if it be possible to render ourselves miserable by aspiring to an independence that nature forbids, it is also possible to be made unhappy by a too obtrusive interference with our individuality.

Of all Christian countries, individuality, as connected with habits, is perhaps the most encouraged in England; and of all Christian countries this is the one, perhaps, in which there is the least individuality of the same nature. The latter fact would be extraordinary, could it not be referred to the religious discipline that so much influenced the colonists, and which in a measure supplied the place of law. In communities in which private acts became the subject of publick parochial investigation, it followed as a natural consequence, that men lived under the constant corrective of publick opinion, however narrow, provincial, or prejudiced. This feature of the American character, therefore is to be ascribed, in part, to the fanaticism of our ancestors, and, in part, to the natural tendency in democracies to mistake and augment the authority of the publick.

'They say'

'THEY say,' is the monarch of this country, in a social sense. No one asks 'who says it,' so long as it is believed that 'they say it.' Designing men endeavor to persuade the publick, that already 'they say,' what these designing men wish to be said, and the publick is only too much disposed blindly to join in the cry of 'they say.'

This is another consequence of the habit of defering to the control of the publick, over matters in which the publick has no right to interfere.

Every well meaning man, before he yields his faculties and intelligence to this sort of dictation, should first ask himself 'who' is 'they,' and on what authority 'they say' utters its mandates.

Rumour

THE people of the United States are unusually liable to be imposed on by false rumours. In addition to the causes that exist elsewhere, such as calculated and interested falsehoods, natural frailty, political machinations, and national antipathies may be enumerated many that are peculiar to themselves.

The great number of, and the imperfect organization of the newspaper establishments, as has already been shown, is a principal reason; necessity, in some degree, compelling a manufacture of 'news,' when none exists in reality.

The great extent of the country, the comparative intelligence of the inhabitants, an intelligence that is often sufficient to incite inquiry, but insufficient for discrimination, the habit of forming opinions, which is connected with the institutions, the great ease of the population, which affords time for gossip, and the vast extent of the surface over which the higher intelligence, that can alone rebuke groundless and improbable rumours, is diffused, are so many reasons for the origin and increase of false reports.

Falsehood and truth are known to be inseparable, every where, but as rumour gains by distance, they are necessarily more mixed together in this country, than in regions where the comparative smallness of surface renders contradiction easier.

The frequency and all controlling character of the elections keep rumours of a certain sort in constant circulation, bringing in corruption and design in support of other motives.

The ability to discriminate between that which is true and that which is false, is one of the last attainments of the human mind. It is the result, commonly, of a long and extensive intercourse with mankind. But one may pass an entire life, in a half-settled and half-civilized portion of the world, and not gain as much acquaintance with general things, as is obtained by boys who dwell in regions more populous. The average proportion between numbers and surface in America, is about twelve to the square mile, whereas, it approaches three hundred, in the older countries of Europe! On this single fact depends much more, in a variety of ways, than is commonly believed.

On Religion

As reason and revelation both tell us that this state of being is but a preparation for another of a still higher and more spiritual order, all the interests of life are of comparatively little importance, when put in the balance against the future. It is in this grand fact that we are to seek for the explanations of whatever may strike us as unjust, partial, or unkind in the dispensations of Providence, as these dispensations affect our temporal condition. If there is no pure and abstract liberty, no equality of condition, no equal participation in the things of the world that we are accustomed to fancy good, on remembering the speck of time passed in the present state, the possibility that what to us may seem a curse, may in truth be a blessing, the certainty that prosperity is more corrupting than adversity, we shall find the solution of all our difficulties.

In a religious point of view, it may be permitted to endeavor to improve our temporal condition, by the use of lawful and just means, but it is never proper to repine. Christ, in the parable of the vine dressers, has taught us a sublime lesson of justice, by showing that to the things which are not our own, we can have no just claim. To this obvious truth, may be added the uncertainty of the future, and the ignorance in which we exist of what is good, or what is evil, as respects our own wants.

There is but one true mode of viewing life, either in a religious, or in a philosophical sense, and that is to remember it is a state of probation in which the trials exceed the enjoyments, and that, while it is lawful to endeavor to increase the latter, more especially if of an intellectual and elevated kind, both form but insignificant interests in the great march of time. Whatever may be the apparent inequalities here, and even they are less real than they appear to be, it is certain that we bring nothing with us into the world, and that we take nothing out of it. Every thing around us serves to teach the lesson that, though inequality of condition here is as probably intended for some great end as it is unavoidable, we come from a state of being in which we know of no such law, to go to one that we have divine revelation for believing will render the trifling disparities and the greatest advantages of this life, matters of insignificance, except as they have had an influence on our deportment, characters and faith. It would be just as discreet for a man who is suffering with hunger to murmur at having been created with such a want, while others are feeding, as to repine that another enjoys advantages he cannot possess. In this country, the aim has been to reduce all the factitious inequalities of station, condition, wealth and knowledge, to a state as natural as comports with civilization, and beyond this it exceeds the power of man to go, without returning to the condition of the savage. Let him, then, on whom the world bears hard, seek his consolation in that source which is never drained, and where more contentment is to be found than shadows a throne, or smiles on riches and power. If it be a positive thing to be a gentleman, or a lady, and as much a folly to deny it as to deny that a horse is an animal, it is equally positive that we carry in us a principle of existence that teaches us, however good and pleasant may seem the outward blessings of the world, that there are still blessings of infinitely greater magnitude, that have the additional merit of being imperishable.

The limits and objects of this work neither require, nor admit of very profound dissertations, but a few words on the peculiarities of religion and of religious feeling in America, may not be misplaced.

The causes which led to the establishment of the principal American colonies, have left a deep impression on the character of the nation. In some respects this impression has been for good, in others for evil. Our business is with the latter.

Fanaticism was the fault of the age, at the time our ancestors took possession of the country, and its exaggerations have entailed on their descendants many opinions that are, at the best, of a very equivocal usefulness. These opinions are to be detected by the contracted notions of those who entertain them, and by a general want of that charity and humility, which are the most certain attendants of the real influence of the meek and beneficent spirit of Christ.

In America the taint of sectarianism lies broad upon the land. Not content with acknowledging the supremacy of the Deity, and with erecting temples in his honor, where all can bow down with reverence, the pride and vanity of human reason enter into and pollute our worship, and the houses that should be of God and for God, alone, where he is to be honored with submissive faith, are too often merely schools of metaphysical and useless distinctions. The nation is sectarian, rather than Christian.

Religion's first lesson is humility; its fruit, charity. In the great and sublime ends of Providence, little things are lost, and least of all is he imbued with a right spirit who believes that insignificant observances, subtleties of doctrine, and minor distinctions, enter into the great essentials of the Christian character. The wisest thing for him who is disposed to cavil at the immaterial habits of his neighbor, to split straws on doctrine, to fancy trifles of importance, and to place the man before principles, would be to distrust himself. The spirit of peace is not with him.

The institutions of the country, by wisely breaking down all artificial and unnecessary distinctions, while they have preserved the ordinances necessary to civilized society, have removed the factitious barriers from one particular vice, which, while it belongs to the nature of man, may be termed a besetting sin of this country. We shall conclude this article, therefore, by simply quoting the stern mandate of the tenth commandment: 'The shalt not covet thy neighbor's house; thou shalt not covet thy neighbor's wife; nor his man-servant, nor his maid-servant, nor his ox, nor his ass, nor any thing that is thy neighbor's.

Conclusion

THE inferences to be drawn from the foregoing reasons and facts, admitting both to be just, may be briefly summed up as follows.

No expedients can equalize the temporal lots of men; for without civilization and government, the strong would oppress the weak, and, with them, an inducement to exertion must be left, by bestowing rewards on talents, industry and success. All that the best institutions, then, can achieve, is to remove useless obstacles, and to permit merit to be the artisan of its own fortune, without always degrading demerit to the place it ought naturally to fill.

Every human excellence is merely comparative, there being no good without alloy. It is idle therefore to expect a system that shall exhibit faultlessness, or perfection.

The terms liberty, equality, right and justice, used in a political sense, are merely terms of convention, and of comparative excellence, there being no such thing, in practice, as either of these qualities being carried out purely, according to the abstract notions of theories.

The affairs of life embrace a multitude of interests, and he who reasons on any of them, without consulting the rest, is a visionary unsuited to control the business of the world.

There is a prevalent disposition in the designing to forget the means in the end, and on the part of the mass to overlook the result in the more immediate agencies. The first is the consequence of cupidity; the last of short-sightedness, and frequently of the passions. Both these faults need be vigilantly watched in a democracy, as the first unsettles principles while it favors artifice, and the last is substituting the transient motives of a day, for the deliberate policy and collected wisdom of ages.

Men are the constant dupes of names, while their happiness and well-being mainly depend on things. The highest proof a community can give of its fitness for self government, is its readiness in distinguishing between the two; for frauds, oppression, flattery and vice, are the offspring of the mistakes.

It is a governing principle of nature, that the agency which can produce most good, when perverted from its proper aim, is most productive of evil. It behoves the well-intentioned, therefore, vigilantly to watch the tendency of even their most highly prized institutions, since that which was established in the interests of the right, may so easily become the agent of the wrong.

The disposition of all power is to abuses, nor does it at all mend the matter that its possessors are a majority. Unrestrained political authority, though it be confided to masses, cannot be trusted without positive limitations, men in bodies being but an aggregation of the passions, weaknesses and interests of men as individuals.

It is as idle to expect what is termed gratitude, in a democracy, as from any other repository of power. Bodies of men, though submitting to human impulses generally, and often sympathetic as well as violent, are seldom generous. In matters that touch the common feeling, they are avaricious of praise, and they usually visit any want of success in a publick man, as a personal wrong. Thus it is that we see a dozen victories forgotten in a single defeat, an irritable vanity in the place of a masculine pride, and a sensitiveness to opinion, instead of a just appreciation of acts.

Under every system it is more especially the office of the prudent and candid to guard against the evils peculiar to that particular system, than to declaim against the abuses of others. Thus, in a democracy, instead of decrying monarchs and aristocrats, who are impotent, it is wiser to look into the sore spots of the only form of government that can do any practical injury, and to apply the necessary remedies, than to be glorifying ourselves at the expense of charity, common sense, and not unfrequently of truth.

Life is made up of positive things, the existence of which it is not only folly, but which it is often unsafe to deny. Nothing is gained by setting up impracticable theories, but alienating opinion from the facts under which we live, all the actual distinctions that are inseparable from the possession of property, learning, breeding, refinement, tastes and principles, existing as well in one form of government, as in another; the only difference between ourselves and other nations, in this particular, lying in the fact that there are no other artificial distinctions than those that are inseparable from the recognised principles and indispensable laws of civilization.

There is less inequality in the condition of men than outward circumstances would give reason to believe. If refinement brings additional happiness, it also adds point to misery. Fortunately, the high consolations of religion, in which lies the only lasting and true relief from the cares and seeming injustice of the world, are equally attainable, or, if there be a disadvantage connected with this engrossing interest, it is against those whose lots are vulgarly supposed to be the most desirable.

In every corner of the world, on every subject under the sun, Penguin represents quality and variety – the very best in publishing today.

For complete information about books available from Penguin – including Pelicans, Puffins, Peregrines and Penguin Classics – and how to order them, write to us at the appropriate address below. Please note that for copyright reasons the selection of books varies from country to country.

In the United Kingdom: Please write to *Dept E.P., Penguin Books Ltd, Harmondsworth, Middlesex, UB7 0DA*

If you have any difficulty in obtaining a title, please send your order with the correct money, plus ten per cent for postage and packaging, to *PO Box No 11, West Drayton, Middlesex*

In the United States: Please write to *Dept BA, Penguin, 299 Murray Hill Parkway, East Rutherford, New Jersey 07073*

In Canada: Please write to *Penguin Books Canada Ltd, 2801 John Street, Markham, Ontario L3R 1B4*

In Australia: Please write to the *Marketing Department, Penguin Books Australia Ltd, P.O. Box 257, Ringwood, Victoria 3134*

In New Zealand: Please write to the *Marketing Department, Penguin Books (NZ) Ltd, Private Bag, Takapuna, Auckland 9*

In India: Please write to *Penguin Overseas Ltd, 706 Eros Apartments, 56 Nehru Place, New Delhi, 110019*

In Holland: Please write to *Penguin Books Nederland B.V., Postbus 195, NL–1380AD Weesp, Netherlands*

In Germany: Please write to *Penguin Books Ltd, Friedrichstrasse 10–12, D–6000 Frankfurt Main 1, Federal Republic of Germany*

In Spain: Please write to *Longman Penguin España, Calle San Nicolas 15, E–28013 Madrid, Spain*

In France: Please write to *Penguin Books Ltd, 39 Rue de Montmorency, F-75003, Paris, France*

In Japan: Please write to *Longman Penguin Japan Co Ltd, Yamaguchi Building, 2–12–9 Kanda Jimbocho, Chiyoda-Ku, Tokyo 101, Japan*